OPERANATOMY

ALFRED ALEXANDER

The First Edition (2,500 copies) of this book
was published by Orion, and printed in Italy in April 1971
Second Edition printed in Great Britain in 1974 for
Crescendo Publishing Company, Boston
by arrangement with Grant & Cutler Ltd.

ISBN 0875-97-091-5

Distributors outside the United States and Canada:
Grant & Cutler Ltd.,
11 Buckingham Street, Strand, London, WC2. Tel.: 01-839 3136

First printed 1971 in Messina Italy, at the Tipo-litho "Cristo Re"
in 12 pt. Janson.
Reprinted 1974 by Redington & Co. London, and typeset by
C. E. Dawkins (Typesetters) Ltd. London in Imprint Series.

ALFRED ALEXANDER

OPERANATOMY

AN ECLECTIC INTRODUCTION TO THE ART OF
THE CONDUCTOR, INSTRUMENTALIST, COMPOSER
PRODUCER, AND TO SCORE READING.
ANALYSIS OF SOUND, SINGER, LIBRETTO AND
PUBLIC, AND ADJUDICATION OF THE CRITIC

CRESCENDO   PUBLISHING   COMPANY   BOSTON

By the same author

Giovanni Verga's La Lupa, Philosophical Publishing House, London, 1968

The Stornello and its Flowers, *Biologia Culturale*, Rome, 1969

Luigi Capuana's Comparatico: a story which made literary history, Ciranna, Rome, 1970

Il comparatico di Luigi Capuana e gl'inizi del verismo (con traduzione inglese), Collana di Narrativa, Ciranna, Rome, 1970

Giovanni Verga, A great writer and his world, Grant & Cutler Ltd., London, 1972

FOREWORD

The demand for all forms of music, and in particular for opera, which has so greatly increased during the years since the end of the war, has brought in its wake a spate of introductory literature.

The operatic works of all important composers have been chronicled and explained in great detail; synopses of plots of a multitude of operas have been published in collected editions, and any theatre programme contains notes giving the historic background of the work being performed, as well as biographical details of past and present executants.

In spite of this wealth of literature, a good deal of the information this book sets out to provide, has not been readily available before.

The object of the book is to further the enjoyment of opera by examining various aspects of its component structure, and to offer simple explanations for terms of sound and music, whose current expositions are none too easy to find, and often difficult to understand.

I am aware of the great difficulty which confronts any attempt to address a public whose musical background is, of necessity, one of great diversity and I sincerely hope that this book can be enjoyed by the comparative newcomer to opera, while still offering points of interest to the experienced musician.

It is dedicated to the many friends who, knowingly and unknowingly, have helped me to write it.

FOREWORD
TO THE SECOND EDITION

My book, a Cenerentola to begin with, has in true operatic style found its Don Ramiro in a public which has welcomed it with unexpected approbation.

Reprinting offered the opportunity to correct errors, remedy blemishes, and to add some items of information. The explanation of the curious term 'English Horn' was inserted, as well as several further libretto examples and remarks about the tonality of the British National Anthem.

A complete new chapter, 'Vocal Technique' now follows the chapter on sound and singer, and a full index of names and works appears at the end of the book.

It is hoped that these additions will be found to be all of a piece with the declared purpose of the book—to further the enjoyment of music in general, and opera in particular.

CONTENTS

FIRST CHAPTER

THE CONDUCTOR

THE CONDUCTOR

In the play *Hiob Praetorius* by Kurt Goetz,* the curtain rises to the sound of orchestral music. In the centre of the stage stands the protagonist in front of a conductor's lectern, his face pale with excitement. He is indulging in his recondite and secret love, he is conducting an orchestra.

The stage directions are quite explicit: 'he conducts the flowing movement of a symphony . . . a lock of hair falls onto his forehead. He marks the entries, encourages the violins, fends off the brass, coaxes the flute. By throwing his head backwards he communicates with the kettle drums. Only at the end of the movement, when he turns the light on from a switch on his lectern, do we become aware that we are not in a concert hall but in a private room and that the orchestra is replaced by an electric gramophone.'

Kurt Goetz's play amusingly exploits for the theatre an ambition which is not at all rare: the secret longing to conduct. In fact, few people who take an interest in music have not at one time or another toyed with the desire to conduct an orchestra. On the face of it, conducting appears straight forward enough, and the rhythmic movements which are visible to the audience do not seem difficult. There is evidence that mere children, even seven-year-olds, have acquitted themselves with distinction in a task which looks much less difficult than playing an instrument or singing. One can go even further and question whether the conductor is really indispensable. It is known that a good orchestra can function quite well on its own; every so often we

---

* Swiss actor and playwright (1888-1960).

read in the newspapers of orchestras which perform serious musical works quite admirably without the aid of a conductor.* This is not altogether surprising: orchestras consist after all of highly competent and experienced musicians who might well be expected to play their parts without any special direction.

The conductor's essential requisites, too, are modest enough. The famous 'baton' is a little stick of wood which can be bought quite cheaply, or made at home by anyone who knows how to use a pocket knife on a piece of wood from copse or hedgerow. A conductor's lectern is neither expensive nor indispensable: any music stand will do in its stead.

To those who see conducting in this light, it comes as a surprise that of all the arts of reproductive musicianship the conductor's part is by far the most difficult one to master. However difficult it may be to play a musical instrument expertly, it is far, far more difficult to become a competent conductor.

The biblical story of Jacob's marriage, which eventually required not less than three consecutive periods of seven years of service, provides a fitting allegory for the conductor's years of toil in pursuit of the mastery of his profession. The first seven years he has to spend learning to play a musical instrument, the piano for preference. When this task is accomplished, he has to labour another seven years, studying the theory of music, the rules of harmony and counterpoint, and the craft of composing. He also has to become reasonably proficient in playing a second instrument, so that he can sit in the orchestra pit and gain experience at the receiving end of the conductor's baton. Finally, the young conductor has to serve a third term of seven years during which he must become competent in score reading and acquire a thorough knowledge of musical literature. He has to study the possibilities and limits of the human voice and of all

---

* During the early 20th century, conductorless orchestras existed in New York, in Moscow (1925) and in Budapest. Since 1960 several conductorless chamber orchestras have successfully established themselves, e.g. the Academy of St. Martin-in-the-Fields.

orchestral instruments. He has to learn the history of music and become proficient in accompanying, as well as in helping the singer to interpret musical phrasing. Only then can he feel certain that he possesses the essential requirements for his calling.

Few professions require an apprenticeship of 21 years. The title 'maestro', which is not legally protected, is more difficult to achieve than many of the legally protected academic titles; yet not even this long period of training and learning will guarantee him a prosperous livelihood or professional success.

To those of his personal friends who enjoy music as amateurs, he certainly is the perfect companion, capable of displaying an ability which, to most music lovers, is as inexplicable as it is fascinating. Friendship with a singer is, for people who are keen on singing, undoubtedly a delightful experience. Similarly, a friend who can play the viola or the cello will be found a great asset, if interest is centred on chamber music. For the sheer enjoyment of music though, nothing ranks higher than the pleasure of having a conductor as a friend. With miraculous facility, music seems to flow reflex-like from his ears into his fingers. Not a single line of written music does he need to fill the room with the fullest sound a piano can produce. Unhesitatingly and with undreamed-of perfection he can play by heart any piece of music his listeners have ever heard, as well as many, many they have never heard before.

Success among his circle of friends does not assure him of success with the public. The reasons for popular success in conducting are as irrational as the reasons for success in other fields. Many excellent musicians and highly competent conductors have failed to achieve it. The element of luck plays an important part, and a conductor's 'popular appeal' is linked as little, or as much, to professional excellence as is popular appeal in any other sphere. No one can explain why one particular officer during the last war appealed to the public so much that he became an immensely popular Field Marshal. The popularity of a conductor's baton is not based on more predictable, or on more valid, reasons than the popularity of a Field Marshal's baton: all depends on the appealing personality.

In the conductor's professional 'armamentarium', personal appeal plays beyond doubt an important part. According to Richard Wagner, only two requirements are essential for a good conductor: to be able to give clearly and unmistakably the right time, and to possess personality.

A person entitled to call himself maestro must be as competent to perform the conductor's work as a qualified doctor must be competent to treat sick patients. However, professional competence and the indefinable trait of possessing 'personality' do not necessarily go together. Personality manifests itself more readily outside the direct field of professional competence. Such supernumerary qualities are of particular importance to the conductor, particularly those qualities which assist him to assert his authority over other people.

The authority over others has in the conductor a peculiarly two-sided aspect. The conductor can decide how the written music should sound, and is in full control of the way the music emerges from the work which is being performed. He is entitled to impose his wishes and his views on those taking part in the performance. He can insist that the sounds which we hear are the sounds he has heard in his own mind's ear; everyone must obey him and submit to his will. He is absolute and complete master, but in order to be a good master, he must at the same time be a good servant. Every instrumentalist and every singer who is taking part in the performance is entitled to rely on his services. They are as much entitled to his serving leadership as he is entitled to their obedience.

This serving leadership is not easily defined; it is an aspect of conducting which is as closely connected with personality as it is with knowledge. It is a leadership executed with baton and hand, with body and eye, with a smile or a frown. To achieve perfect results, and to obtain the best response from those he leads, an indefinable rapport of affection and of mutual encouragement is necessary. He must *like* the artists who perform 'for him' and they must, in a feeling of innocent love, like and admire him. It is rather puzzling why this peculiar feeling of attachment should be required, but it is just as essential to his best work, as it is essential for the best work of a surgeon that he and the theatre sister should share a feeling of innocent affection for one another.

A conductor can, of course, only render his services properly if he has full mastery over the score. He must know the score in all its details, and know it virtually by heart. He can refresh his memory by looking at it from time to time, but if he has his nose too much in the score* he will be physically unable to fulfil his duties. He should *in fact* conduct by heart, though he should *not* conduct without a score. Most singers dislike the absence of the score from the conductor's lectern. Singers feel that they are more 'at risk', more *personally* exposed than the conductor is. They feel that if the conductor's memory lapses it would harm them more than it would harm *him*. This feeling is appreciated by sensitive conductors: by mischance, the score of *Tannhäuser* was once substituted for that of *Lohengrin*, but with complete composure the conductor turned the score's pages over at suitable intervals of ten or twenty pages, as conductors often do, in order not to alarm his singers.

The instrumentalist expects from the conductor a clear indication of the rhythm, though it is up to the conductor to choose the way he decides to beat. Richard Strauss, for example, favoured a very slow beat, and tended to give fewer beats to a bar than most conductors.† Apart from a clear beat, the instrumentalist is entitled to expect a slight nod or a movement of

---

* The bon mot that 'the conductor must have the score in his head in order not to have his head in the score,' has been attributed to many conductors.

† According to Leo Wurmser (see also p. 23) he would beat the 6/8 Andantes in Mozart's Prague and G minor Symphonies in two, the slow movement of Beethoven's Fourth Symphony in three, the first movement of the 'Pastoral' Symphony in one, all the 4/4 or 12/8 sections of the Adagio from the Ninth Symphony in four, and 'Là ci darem la mano' from *Don Giovanni* in two.

the left hand to mark his solo entries, particularly those which are exposed or lend themselves to mistakes.

The singer, too, is entitled to this service, or rather to even more: he expects the conductor to 'breathe with him'. It is often difficult for the singer to know exactly how long to hold a note, and a signal to this effect, sometimes carried out by a slight movement of the shoulder, can be a very welcome aid. Breathing with the singer has other advantages as well. It prevents the conductor from choosing a tempo which would be uncomfortable for the singer. The singer's comfort ranks high on the considerate conductor's list of priorities, and should influence the selection of tempi. A tempo which does not give the singer adequate time to enunciate his words is bound to be too fast, even if instrumentally it sounds attractive.

It is not always possible, or even desirable, to sing a phrase precisely in the timing in which it is written. Many singers like to take slight liberties with the time values of their notes in order to style a phrase more convincingly, or to enable them to show certain characteristics of their voice to better advantage. This is quite permissible in some works, and they rightly expect the conductor to accompany them and to accept their own timing for the rhythm of the orchestra. The conductor will follow this lead, but must on the other hand firmly discourage singers from the exaggeration of such liberties, and in works in which it is not appropriate avoid this type of effect altogether. Without leaving the singer high and dry, he must make quite sure that a singer who is fascinated by his own voice does not 'sit' too much on his sounds: the foremost loyalty of the conductor must always be to the composer.

Far more often than not, the composer is dead and the conductor has become his acting trustee, the single custodian of the 'loyalty to the work' (*Werktreue*). This concept has in recent times assumed increasing importance and strongly influences our attitude to works of past periods. It is a comparatively new conception, on the whole a practice of the 20th century, and it needs explanation.

During the 19th century the performance of works dating from previous periods was almost invariably governed by contemporary sentiment. Everything was rendered not only in sympathy with the mood of the period in which it was being reproduced, but also within the full feeling of it. This attitude caused many musical works to suffer quite serious distortions.

During the 20th century the idea of *Werktreue* started to take root, and the desire to render works of past periods in the spirit in which they were conceived became so strong that it almost swelled to a passion. On the face of it, this seems commendable and justifiable enough. However, it has to be borne in mind that even at the best of times true loyalty to the work is possible only in a rather limited way. The true acoustic impressions of the performances of the past are unfortunately irretrievable and nothing can bring their sound back: neither our studies of the conditions of old performances, nor our knowledge of the structure of the orchestras, and not even the use of reproductions of old instruments, can achieve this result. In fact, it was found that the extremes of *Werktreue* resulted in performances which sounded historically biased. This led to the realization that a performance of unattractive dryness may well result if too little contemporary sentiment is allowed to enter into it. Desirable as the conception of loyalty to the work appears *in principle*, we have learnt that exaggerated fidelity has a similar effect to that of infidelity. This may sound surprising, but it can be to some extent exemplified by referring to the recitative of opera.

Baroque opera featured two, the *recitativo accompagnato* in which the whole or part of the orchestra accompanied the singer's words, and the *recitativo secco* (dry) where the accompanying chords were played on the harpsichord.

The harpsichord stems from the 16th century and was for over 200 years the most widely distributed keyboard instrument. Its sound is produced by *plucking* a string (originally with a raven's quill) and for this reason it is *not* a direct ancestor of the piano. The piano's direct ancestor is the clavichord, a keyboard instrument whose beginnings lie in the 15th century. (See also p. 141.)

Many conductors like to accompany the *recitativo secco* themselves, and as the revival of the harpsichord is a comparatively recent phenomenon, conductors until not very long ago would accompany the *secco* unashamedly on the piano.* This was a musical anachronism: the piano's use for this purpose would now raise an outcry, as we appreciate that the harpsichord's short, sharp sounds are eminently suitable for the *secco's* accompaniment.

In using instruments of the past, we can produce the sounds of a past period, but these sounds cannot make us *hear* what our forebears heard. We can no longer perceive the harpsichord in the same way as our ancestors did, because the sound of the present piano's 'hammer power' has conditioned our brain: it has changed our relative acoustic sensitivity towards those fixed-tone instruments which preceded it.

The conditioning by sounds in relation to subsequent acoustic sensations is now well recognized, and is made important use of in the acoustic education of children with defective hearing. This conditioning of our brain also suggests that the current notion that Bach's 'Klavier Music', originally composed for the harpsichord and the clavichord, must not be played on a piano, is quite justified on historic grounds, but certainly not justifiable in physiological terms.

Similar arguments apply also to others of the revivified old instruments and to their orchestral use. It is up to the conductor to use his taste and knowledge in order to steer the work safely between the Scylla and Charybdis of such potentially conflicting loyalties.

The judgement of how far the conductor wishes to extend his loyalty to the work, is only one of the decisions he has to make. He also has to decide on his loyalty to the composer, a decision which may well force him deliberately to vary firmly

---

* A fairly recent recording of *Don Giovanni* retains this feature.

entrenched usages, even if they originate from the period of the composer himself. He may in fact have to become more papal than the pope. The rhythmic freedom for instance, the *rubamento di tempi*, may well have been a composer's wish, or been the custom of the composer's time. The composer may or may not have made notes to this effect in the score. The conductor must not permit his singers too much liberty in this respect and he has to search his own heart as well.

The present trend is for strict adherence to the composer's imagined wish, independent of previous customs, even if the custom dates from the period of the composer. Mozart's operas were, for instance, during his own period and for many decades after, subject to quite elaborate *rubati* (*rubato* means *stolen*). The conductor is the ultimate judge of what rhythmic freedom a singer may be entitled to, or a work may be submitted to. He must prevent other people's excesses diplomatically, and avoid his own firmly.

In order to understand the reasons as well as the pattern for the visible movements of conducting, a short account of its historic development is necessary.

To 'conduct' means to guide, and the need for guidance in music has existed ever since the days of primitive music-making with drums and flutes. Right from its beginnings, conducting had to fulfil a double task: it had to keep the music 'together' from the rhythmic point of view, and it had to inspire and animate the musicians.

Before the existence of written music, it was a further task of the conductor to indicate the pitch of the sounds the musicians were meant to sing or to play. This necessity produced a craft of its own, the 'cheironomy', and cheironomy can therefore be regarded as the precursor of conducting. It consisted essentially of hand signals relating to the *pitch* of sound. The method is, to a certain extent, comparable to those hand signals which are taught to the completely deaf in order to designate the *type* of sound. In the middle ages, the rhythm of the music was generally conveyed by knocking on the floor with a stick or by waving a rag. Later on, waving a violin bow served the same purpose. From the historical point of view, the indication of the rhythm was obviously by far the more necessary of the two essential elements of conducting, and was much more urgently required than any spiritual encouragement.

The composer of early music was generally also its conductor. In the 17th century, conducting was done from the harpsichord. Conducting with a baton only became the rule after the *continuo* or figured bass had been abandoned and the harpsichord become unnecessary.

The 19th century saw the full separation of composer and conductor, most explicitly perhaps in the person of Hans von Bülow, who is regarded as the father of modern conducting. Gradually, after prolonged trial and effort, characteristic methods of beating were developed, or rather developed themselves. Different beating for 4/4, 3/4 rhythm, etc. as well as for the marking of pauses (*fermate*) emerged. However, due to the immense progress of modern instrumentalists in musical education, experience and efficiency, these signals have now lost much of their importance. Most musicians are at present rhythmically so perfectly schooled that they no longer need explicit signals. This gives the conductor a freer hand, and enables him to keep the rhythm fully under control by merely hinting at the time values. Explicit signals are now far more important for school or amateur conducting than they are for serious musical work.

The exact manner as well as the type of the bodily movements the conductor chooses to make in order to maintain the necessary rapport is now largely governed by his own wishes and by his own feelings. The physical actions which follow are therefore an expression of his own personality, and this results in the fact that, although the basic movements, with minimal modifications, are the same for everyone, the manner of beating differs significantly among different conductors. The extent of the downbeat, of the upbeat, and of the 'ictus' (the critical point of the conductor's beat), can vary from one conductor to another to such an extent that no specific rules for the detail of the movements apply any longer. For the singer as well as for the instrumentalists it is essential to observe and to 'tune in' to the conductor. Only after this tuning in has taken place during the rehearsals does the conductor's approach become clear.

It is easy enough to understand that music invites, or even enforces, rhythmic movements of the conductor's body. In the interest of general aesthetics, a moderation of movement is, on the whole, desirable. Some conductors delight in imitating the tonic-clonic convulsions of an epileptic seizure, indulge in unnecessary bobbings up and down (the dance music in *Carmen* seems particularly apt to provoke such excesses), and in closing their eyes, or in floor-scrubbing mimes reminiscent of 'Mrs. Mopp'. Others go to the opposite extreme and limit the movement of their hands to what is sometimes referred to as 'knitting', a movement considered indecisive by singers and musicians.

It is often assumed that an excess of movement looks interesting from the audience's point of view, or conversely that a lack of visible movement may appear uninteresting. Richard Strauss' conducting, particularly in his later years, was characterized by a deliberate restraint of movement, possibly caused by a desire to conserve his energy.

Leo Wurmser,* who had frequently worked with Richard Strauss, has recorded certain incidents connected with this restraint:

"Strauss' conducting may often have looked uninteresting to the audience—he did not care what impression his gestures made on them—but seen from the stage or the orchestra pit it was quite another matter. With him it was the baton, in fact the tip of the baton, that was all-important. Usually he would beat from the wrist only, keeping his right arm close to his body and raising it only for big climaxes. As for his left arm, it generally remained still (not necessarily in his waistcoat pocket, as he wrote

---

* Leo Wurmser, a fine musician and conductor, who had remained almost unknown, died in 1967. The above extract from his broadcast 'Notes about Strauss' is quoted by kind permission of the B.B.C.

in his advice to young conductors), but he used his left hand mainly to keep down the brass or other groups of instruments, or to give an occasional entry; though even these things he preferred to do with his eyes, which were large and blue and extremely expressive. It was quite extraordinary to watch how a tightening of the muscles of his shoulders would indicate a forte or crescendo, or how by a glance he could give a player his cue or indicate that he was too loud or too soft. Strauss himself has described his manner of conducting as 'conducting with one's eyes' or 'conducting with one's tie'. The latter remark was, of course, made with his tongue in his cheek, for he had a strong sense of humour which frequently revealed itself. For instance, one day I heard him rehearse the *Oberon* overture. When he came to the last bar of the Adagio, where the violas sustain the E and D, he beat a very small sub-divided 4, keeping his baton in front of his chest; no fortissimo chord came, so he said, 'But gentlemen, why don't you play the fortissimo chord?' The leader replied, 'Herr Doktor, you didn't give us an upbeat.' And Strauss, with a broad grin said, 'Ah, but we mustn't let the audience know a quaver in advance that a crash is coming,' and he rehearsed the two bars until the orchestra played the fortissimo chord following his pianissimo beat and was as pleased as a child when it came off."

The musical knowledge and musical education of the conductor have to be much more thorough than those of the instrumentalist or singer. Many conductors are capable of playing several musical instruments as expertly as any of the musicians in the orchestra under their command. Some masterly players of stringed instruments like to conduct on occasions, and have established secondary reputations for themselves as highly sensitive conductors, particularly of works connected with their own speciality.

Another point of interest deserves mentioning in this connection. The virtuoso violin or piano player finds himself immersed in an immense repertory of all styles of music. The oboist's, or even the cellist's solo-literature is, on the other hand, somewhat limited and eventually becomes almost too familiar to him. The true artist's irrepressible desire for new means of expression is thus somewhat thwarted, and this can cause the 'small repertory complex', a feeling of restriction which affects even the most successful. Conducting can provide an ideal remedy, and restore the artist's musical equilibrium.

Occasionally, a great master conductor arises out of the orchestra pit. Toscanini was a cello player, and Rudolf Kempe is an ex-oboist. Colin Davis is an ex-clarinet player, and it is not surprising that the intimate link between conductor and orchestra is one of his special aims.

The conductor does not need a singing voice, though most conductors sing, or rather mime with their voices, not only the sound of the vocal line but that of every conceivable instrument as well. Even in gramophone recordings, conductors can occasionally be heard to sing, and when Pablo Casals, at the age of 93, conducted one of his own compositions, he was reported to have sung vigorously. In fact, conductors often sing loudly during rehearsals, perhaps less loudly at performances, and even during recording sessions they can rarely resist the urge to hum.

This is not surprising, and is possibly a general sign of deep involvement with the music. However, it may well be that one of his past duties has greatly stimulated this instinct in the conductor.

The young maestro is expected to join an opera company as a repetiteur, and as such he has to conduct preliminary orchestral rehearsals and to prepare singers in readiness for their work with the opera's conductor. Additionally, it is one of his duties to act as a prompter, which, in opera, is a very important assignment; it forms an aspect of operatic tradition in which Italian and German tradition differ significantly, and, over the years, two patterns of prompting have emerged. In Italian usage the *suggeritore* acts as a secondary conductor, and, apart from giving the singers their cues, he sings or shouts every important word in its exact musical setting. In German operatic usage, the role is less significant and is restricted to giving the singers the cue words of the libretto, ahead of their place in the score.

In any case—though more so in the Italian style—the prompter's work is essential for the singer, and all the more so in cases where the conductor's beat is not very clear and explicit. The public are little aware of it all, because the secondary conductor is generally *not* listed on the programme and his activities are not visible. Only if the producing style excludes the use of a prompter's box (as in the production of *The Knot Garden* at Covent Garden) and the secondary conductor has to work from the pit, can he be seen by the audience.

Prompting forms an important stage of a conductor's career and gives him a thorough knowledge of the vocal line, and of the words of the libretto; it may well stimulate his natural tendency to sing.

The conductor does not need absolute (perfect) pitch hearing—some musicians believe that perfect pitch hearing can at times be a nuisance—but his relative pitch hearing must be infallible. The conductor's 'musicality' which pre-supposes a discerning hearing acuity of well above normal (i.e. average) standards, with an immediate sensitivity to quarter-tone tolerances,* must be exemplary and at no time whatever open to doubt. Such requisites, which are essential to him, place him musically well above the average level of the musicians and singers under his command. His musical gifts alone must entitle him to their fullest respect.

This respect is, at the beginning, accorded to him automatically, as is evidenced by some rehearsal customs. Musicians, particularly singers, generally use among themselves christian names almost at once. Completely disregarding national differences and artistic standing, singers who find themselves together immediately address one another with great familiarity. Out of natural respect for the maestro, no singer, however famous, will address a conductor by his christian name. Even if friendship develops, formal terms will be resumed during actual work. A conductor who is treated with such respect as his natural due,

---

* It is reliably reported that Mozart's hearing enabled him readily to discern one-sixth tone tolerances, i.e. 33 *cent* (see page 140).

must of course prove it to be justified if he wishes to maintain his authority. It is at times impossible to avoid disappointing *someone*, particularly in the performing arts, but woe betide the conductor who disappoints too many too often. Once respect for him has gone, he will find it very difficult to obtain worthwhile results.

Respect is never easily maintained. A conductor's behaviour is permanently and relentlessly scrutinized, and if he succumbs to error it can prove a serious hazard for him. The casting of operatic roles is, or should be, one of the conductor's prerogatives. This activity is fraught with particular pitfalls. No one expects a conductor to be a saint or to remain impervious to female charm, but he should not too obviously exhibit signs of 'sopranophilia', an occupational disease to which the conductor is as prone as the boiler-maker is to deafness. Whatever turmoil a singer's voice or appearance may cause in his heart, his impartiality in casting must not only remain unaffected, but must clearly be shown to have remained unaffected. Disregard of this principle can result in a serious loss of authority, a very severe penalty for him to pay. Every conductor must be aware that he is in the public's eye, and while he may well bask in that heroworship and adoration which the public is prepared to offer him, he must always remember that he is treading on dangerous ground.

In its unceasing search for personalities who are suitable for glorification, the public tends to admire excessively and is inclined to credit its heroes with superhuman qualities even in their private lives. True greatness in a special field is not infrequently linked with great character traits as well. Quite apart from his musical qualities, Toscanini, for instance, has given the world an example of intrepid behaviour when he refused to yield to political temptation and exiled himself from his homeland rather than let his musical gifts aid political tyranny. Such fortitude is however rare, and some conductors were only too delighted to beat the rhythm of the tyrants' tunes.

It is unreasonable to expect perfection in one's favourite

conductor and it is equally unreasonable to perpetuate recrimin-
ations regarding past shortcomings.

It was perhaps unavoidable that the revolutionary improvement in global communications, and the complete change of
reward-potential which the post-war years with their almost
insatiable demand for music have created, should have made their
mark on conducting as well. A type of conductor is beginning to
arise who, aware of his value in the musical common market, is
showing signs of the hard-headed, big-business executive's
mentality. One can only hope that these will remain isolated
occurrences, and that the more old-fashioned, somewhat romantic figure of the great conductor will continue to emerge from
among the coming generations. On the whole, the highly
successful conductor has so many demands to meet, and so much
to know and to do, that he should not really have to face business
problems as well.

In addition to all the things musical he has to master, in
addition to the need for helpful psychological insight into the
problems of others and the necessity to adapt his behaviour to the
gaze of a curious public, the conductor is also faced with a serious
language problem. A singer may well sing the sounds and words
of a language 'phonetically', even if he does not understand
them: the conductor cannot avail himself of such practices. He
has to understand the libretto and he has to communicate with
foreign artists. In other words, he has to have a practical knowledge of the main operatic languages, i.e. of Italian, German and
French. A working knowledge of Russian and Spanish offers
further advantages, but is not essential.

Knowledge of the Italian language was once regarded as
essential for every musician. All musical directions are by tradition written in Italian, and Italian was at the end of the 18th
century as indispensable for music as French was for diplomacy
at the end of the 19th century. Full understanding of the meaning
of musical markings can have practical advantages as well. A
cellist on tour in Italy, who found himself prevented from taking
his cello into the passengers' compartment because the guard

insisted on it being placed in the luggage van, was filled with great apprehension for the safety of his precious instrument. He remembered Beethoven's directions to the Adagio of op. 18 no. 6, and wrote the words: 'Questo pezzo si deve trattare con la più gran delicatezza' (This piece has to be handled with the utmost gentleness) on the cello case.

In his triad of foreign languages, Italian is for the conductor the most important one. Unfortunately, it is generally also the most difficult one to learn. For reasons which are linguistically and psychologically not fully understood, Italian and English contain reciprocally inhibiting factors. There are surprisingly few English people about who speak Italian well, and equally few Italian people who can speak really good English. This does not apply to musical life only; even in Britain's Foreign Office which, in its higher echelons, is linguistically as fine a body as can be found anywhere, the knowledge of Italian is rather limited.

German, because of its greater affinity with English, presents much less difficulty. Although Italian grammar is much easier than German, it was found during the last war that troops stationed in Germany could learn during the same amount of time much more of German than British troops in Italy could learn of Italian. As an operatic language, French is not quite as important as the other two, and the fact that practically everyone educated in this country possesses schoolboy French is of help.

Even though it would prove to be a great asset, it is not necessary, nor could it reasonably be expected, that a conductor should speak three foreign languages perfectly. He must, however, have more than a 'smattering' and he must know enough of those languages to be able to resist the temptation of translating phonetically. To some extent, English, French, Italian and German are all European vernaculars which share a Latin inheritance, though they have made very different use of their Latin heritage. Phonetic translations are, therefore, fraught with unexpected dangers, and the word 'conductor' itself is not a bad example to demonstrate the pitfalls of phoney phonetics. In Italian, the conductor is called *direttore* (*d'orchestra*), in German he is the *Dirigent* and in French the *chef* (*d'orchestre*). A chart of the misunderstandings which lie in wait for the phonetic translator is given here:

	Conductor	**Direttore**	**Chef**	**Dirigent**
English Significance:	**Conductor**	Director	Male Cook	Ingredient of a Medicine
Italian Phonetic Equivalents	CONDUTTORE		CHEF	DIRIGENTE
Italian Significance:	Tram or Bus Driver	**Conductor**	Senior Police Officer	General Manager of a Public Utility Company
French Phonetic Equivalent:	CONDUCTEUR	DIRECTEUR		DIRIGEANT
French Significance:	Guide	Headmaster	**Conductor**	Pertaining to the upper class
German Phonetic Equivalent:	KONDUKTEUR	DIREKTOR	CHEF	
German Significance:	Fare Collector	Bank Manager	Departmental Head	**Conductor**

Nothing can save the conductor from having to know his languages—all the more reason to respect and admire his versatility.

His training, of course, is not for nothing, and to conduct a good operatic performance is no mean reward. The longing for power is deeply anchored in the human mind. Few achieve it, but the conductor has achieved it and exercises his supreme power at each performance. Before the performance begins, he can reflect that all the famous people he conducts are his marionettes, and that they will do as *he* wills them. They may well sparkle tonight, but they sparkle in *his* sky.

The evening has arrived. He has looked at some passages in the score and thought, even while changing, of all the little items he may still have to confirm with his singers. A short time before the performance he visits his principal singers in their dressing-rooms. They are more exposed than he is, and suffer more from tension, anxiety and stage-fright than he does. For him it is easier to feel collected and to appear cool, and he must use this advantage to inspire confidence and courage.

Contact with his artists is close, the mutual link is strongly felt: they work for him. When he approaches his beautiful soprano's dressing-room, he sees the man she loves leaving her little room and is just in time to overhear their farewell. "I'll sing for *you*", she says to him, as sopranos are inclined to say to the men they love, to the men they imagine they love—and to those they wish to persuade that they love.

For the man in love with a singer, this is indeed the sweetest sound, the *dolcissimo* of her voice, but the conductor only smiles to himself: this 'I'll sing for *you*' means nothing, and if she has any sense, she knows it, too.* Whomever she may be in love with, her voice will only sound perfect if she sings for one man only, and that man is her conductor.

---

* If she really thinks of a person she is in love with while she is singing, she is in danger of sounding sentimental or *schmaltzy* (from *schmalzig*, a recent loan word of 20th century Viennese slang, meaning *greasy*). Schmalz = grease.

The performance ends. He feels exhilarated and exhausted at the same time. The physical effort alone, so unremitting throughout the whole evening, has been tiring. He has taken his curtain call and has kissed his soprano's hand. The singers expect him to praise them, or at least to smile forgivingly. The applause has ceased and the audience are leaving. The stage is curiously quiet, and its acoustics have suddenly changed. Everyone chats for a few minutes, but he leaves soon, a little aloof. In his room he can keep himself to himself; only those he really wants to see may dare to approach him, but, first of all—away with that sweaty shirt!

Fatigue makes itself felt soon. Unwinding is always a problem, but much less for him than it is for the singers, who visit one another in their untidy little rooms and sip a glass of champagne with their friends, traditionally out of the weirdest assortment of mugs, paper cups and old wine glasses.

He does not share the feeling of relief which they now experience.

During the performance he has driven the engine relentlessly. He has *heard* it misfire now and again, but just that, and no *more* than that; he had to go on and there was no time to think back. During the scene-changes too, when he was waiting for the signal light on his lectern to come on, he only thought *forwards*. Somehow, however, he managed to store the recollection of all the little 'slips', and now they come to his mind again and force him to think of what went wrong, and what he can do to prevent such things from happening again. Even at its most enjoyable, life means incessant work.

Yet is their pride but labour and sorrow!

THE A B C
OF SCORE READING

THE ABC OF SCORE READING

Scores are of comparatively recent origin. The earliest scores date from about 1650, though already in the 16th century musical lines were printed one above the other, thus initiating the vertical notation of music. The score's syntax and grammar are the laws of harmony and of counterpoint.

The laws of harmony govern the rules according to which chords should follow one another, rules which have been of the greatest importance for the teaching and execution of music since 1600. Perfect acquaintance with these laws was essential for the playing of the *continuo*, or figured bass. In this method, the permanent bass accompaniment was written as a single line of notes which were supplemented by figures. This formed a sort of 'musical shorthand', understandable only to those who were fully familiar with the rules of harmony.

Counterpoint (*punctus contra punctum*, point against point, i.e. note against note) was the art of accompanying a *cantus firmus* with a second, third and fourth voice. The *cantus firmus* (i.e. the fixed tune) or *cantus prius factus* (i.e. the previously made tune) was the melody which formed the basis of a given piece of music, and was either newly invented or taken from an existing source. The accompanying notes did not need to correspond in their time values to those of the *cantus firmus*, but could move in a different manner. They had to fulfil the two roles of making sense by themselves, and of blending with the other lines *harmoniously*, i.e. in conformity with the rules of harmony. Counterpoint, therefore, relates to the 'horizontal' in the music, but at the same time must always relate to the 'vertical' as well (linear and harmonic counterpoint). In its 1000-year-old history, the use of counterpoint led to many special forms of musical composition. Its apotheosis is the fugue.

Score reading forms the most important part of the conductor's work and is a most complicated craft to master. It is probably the most difficult *routine* activity which can be expected of the human brain.

Only if a voice or an instrument is used on its own (solo), does music ever consist of a simple sound. As soon as more than one instrument or more than one voice participate in the sound, a chord results. Practically all sounds of the orchestra are chords. These chords are presented in the score in vertical order. In order to hear the sound of the chord in his mind's ear, the conductor must be able to convert the vertical line of the score into a 'sound picture'. This process is beset by the most appalling difficulties.

The different instruments are noted on each individual page of the score from top to bottom in a convenient order. The wood-wind comes first, then the brass, then the percussion, afterwards the voices, and finally the stringed instruments.* This seems a good enough arrangement. However, the instruments are noted in differing systems of notation, i.e. in different alphabets (different clefs), as well as in different languages (keys), and in order to convert it all into the same sound language immediate reading of different clefs as well as immediate transposing are necessary.

The system is hopelessly difficult, but the many attempts made at simplification (and theoretically it should be possible to simplify score reading quite considerably) have all foundered. It has even been alleged that composers are opposed to a change in the system because they regard the scores' difficulty as a protection, as a sign of the mysterious and the extraordinary in their work.

The process of immediate assessment of the vertical aspect

---

* Many exceptions to this rule exist. Mozart and Rossini, for instance, often wrote the string parts at the top of the score.

of the score is difficult enough. However, the process has to be repeated in the horizontal progress of the music for every beat of each bar. Vertical reading, therefore, has to be combined with horizontal reading, and score reading can be compared to the rapid reading of a completed crossword puzzle, throughout the whole time the music lasts. Textbooks on score reading reiterate the injunction that 'one has to learn to see with the ear, and hear with the eye', but this old platitude is no real help.

In order to explain the complexities of score reading on a *non*-musical basis, one of the opening passages from the Prelude (preface) to *Androcles and the Lion* by Bernard Shaw has been scored here, in the pattern of the comparatively simple classical orchestra which Beethoven used for his symphonies. It is a passage of 34 words. Each word is noted vertically, and the sentence proceeds horizontally from left to right.

			L				F					R					M			M			P	C
I·		B			B		A		S	O	H			H		H	E	I			O		O	O
		E			I		P					I		I		I	M	L			A	R	L	N
		G			L												N	A					I	S

		I			A	A	U			S			V			L	O			A	C	A	T
	I	N		O	A	R		R			F			I			I	F	D		N	H	N	I
		N			A		E		I			G		C		P	O		H	L	D	U	D	T

T		T						T		T			T										T	U

		I		O		I	B	W		I			I	R	H	H		O		I	H	N	M	I	R	I	T
		N		K		F	B	A			N		S	O	T	A		R		R	I	S	O	T	C	C	I
				O										N		I		E		N	I	I	H	A	O
		G				A	S					N		D	S	E		S	S				E	E	E	L	N
	S					S	S				E		G					S	S				Y	S	S	S	S

To read this passage at speed is difficult enough, but it still does not present anything equal to the real difficulties of score reading. In order to approximate our sample to the complexities of true score reading, we have to make several important changes, the reasons for which have to be explained first.

CLEFS

The difficulties of score reading are due to two facts. The first is that musical notation occurs in different clefs, and the second that the musical instruments are strictly divided into 'C' and 'non C' instruments.

Originally, C was the third step of the scale. It assumed its role as the base of the scale system because no accidentals were necessary for the scale based on it.

Clefs are approximately 1000 years old. The use of different clefs is the result of historical developments, but does still serve practical purposes. The clef's function was to put the centre of the range of instruments (or voices) into a suitable and convenient position on the staff.

The lines of the staff represented originally the strings of the stringed instruments. These lines were put at intervals of the third because this permitted three positions for musical notes: one above, one below and one across the line.

When a staff of more than one line came to be used, its lines were differentiated by different colours. In most instances the F line was red, and the C line green or yellow. Guido d'Arezzo* used four lines and each line had its own clef.

All clefs are derived from letters of the alphabet, and their similarity to ornamental initials in medieval manuscripts is still recognizable.

---

* Guido d'Arezzo (cira. 985–1050) was the inventor of the musical notation on multiple lines as well as of Solmisation, the 'Gamut'.

At least four clefs are still in regular use.

1. The G clef (also violin or treble clef) became fixed on the G line and is used for the flute, the oboe, the clarinet, the horn, the trumpet and the violin, and occasionally for the top of the range of viola and cello.

2. The F clef (bass clef) on the F line, also a fixed clef, is, for more convenient reading, used for the bassoon, the kettle drum, the cello, the double bass, the trombone and the tube.

3. The instrumental alto clef is used for the viola. It is one of the still mobile 'C clefs'.

4. The instrumental tenor clef. This clef is used for the higher reaches of the cello and the bassoon, and sometimes for the tenor trombone. It too is a (mobile) C clef.

C Instruments

The C instrument is an instrument which, in its unadulterated normal form or shape, is capable of sounding the harmonics of C major.

The classical C instrument is the piano, where C major is reflected by the 'all white' (basic) range of keys. Every string instrument can be used as a C instrument. The cello and the viola are on account of their fundamentals the truest C instruments of this group, as the C string is their lowest sound. The violin might have made a good G instrument (the G string is its lowest string) but, like all other stringed instruments, it lends itself perfectly well to use as a C instrument.

Among the wind instruments, the flute, the oboe, the bassoon and the C trumpet as well as the C clarinet are C instruments, and the trombone and the bass tuba are generally treated as if they were C instruments.

The only adjustments which the conductor has to make when he reads parts which are written for C instruments are due to clef usages.

The violin and bass clefs, which are also the standard clefs for the right and the left hand on the piano, do not need explanation.

C Clefs

The C clef is a mobile clef which fixes the 'middle' C on to any desired line of the staff: the clef's centre piece indicates the line or the space of the staff which is to be read as middle C. It is for this reason a very practical clef, and a potential C clef exists for every line and every space of the staff.

The C clefs are divided into 'instrumental' and 'vocal' C clefs. Only two of the instrumental C clefs are still in current use (see above), the viola's alto clef and the instrumental tenor clef.

If one looks at the piano notation (the Grand Staff), one realizes that between its treble and its bass staff one line is missing. The missing line is the middle C line.

If this line is extended, it becomes the centre line of all C clefs.

If we borrow two lines from the treble staff above, and two lines from the bass clef below, the viola clef results.

If we borrow only one line from above and three lines from below, the instrumental tenor clef results.

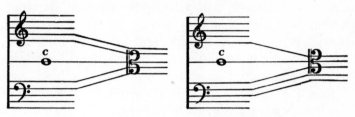

Beginners can memorize it as follows—

Two from above	One from above
Two from below	Three from below
The viola's in the middle	And it's the cello's riddle

The human voice is now almost always regarded as a C instrument, and vocal C clefs are practically obsolete. The tenor's part is almost always written in the violin clef, though it will sound one octave lower. The soprano and alto clefs were replaced by the violin clef as the result of the courageous action of the Milan publisher, Lucca,* who incurred much hostility by using this clef in his scores. He persisted in this practice and eventually forced everyone to follow suit, simplifying thereby the teaching and learning of singing considerably.

NON-C INSTRUMENTS AND THE CROOKS

Non-C instruments are instruments which cannot sound C major as their monther tongue.

Some of the wind instruments (flute, oboe and bassoon and some trumpets), are, as mentioned above, fortunate in this respect, and their natural air column allows them to speak naturally in C. Others are not so lucky. The horn, the English horn, the clarinet, the trumpet and the saxophone just cannot do so. *The reason is that they are wind instruments whose resonance depends upon the length of their air column.* Most of them are old

---

* Francesco Lucca (1802-1872). He was Verdi's publisher until he dared to become Wagner's first publisher in Italy.

instruments, and through hundreds of years of development it has been found that certain lengths of air column have been proved to function more satisfactorily than others. By satisfactory functioning is meant that they cover the range of the desired sounds with tone of good quality, and that they offer the player good and convenient possibilities of execution. The clarinet, for instance, is constructed in such a way that the pitch produced by its basic (open tone) air column is either B flat, or A or E flat. The horn's natural air column produces F, and the trumpet's natural air column B flat.

The obstacles which these natural tunings produce have been gradually overcome during the last 100 or 150 years by the construction of complicated valves. In the time of Haydn, Mozart and Beethoven such valves did not exist. In order to enable non-C instruments to speak in another key, 'crooks', i.e. U-shaped pieces of metal tubing of varying lengths, had to be used, and inserted into the instrument whenever the music modulated. The instrument would then automatically speak in the key of the crook, and accidentals were not necessary in the score. It was sufficient for the composer to name the crook to be used, and inserted into the brass instruments whenever the music really automatic transposers.

TRANSPOSITION

Every non-C instrument needs transposing. For this purpose the conductor has to know what pitch should sound for each note which is printed in his score. *The difference between the written note and the actual sound is called the 'interval of transposition'. Most non-C instruments transpose downwards.*

The best rule for downward transposition is as follows: write the note C and, next to it, the pitch of the instrument designated in the score.

A Instrument   *F Instrument*   *B flat Instrument*

The note C represents the note which the composer has written. The 'letter-name' of the instrument names the sound which is heard when this written note is played. The drop in pitch from the C to the letter-name of the instrument indicates the interval of transposition, and this interval applies to every single sound: every sound will sound as much lower as the transposition interval states. *On the B flat instrument, for instance, each written note will sound one whole tone lower than it was written, and the composer, of course, had to write it one tone higher than he wished it to sound.*

A principle of transposition is also applied in the so-called *scordatura*. This is the deliberate mis-tuning of stringed instruments, including the harp, in order to change their sound-character or to make it feasible to play sounds and chords which it would otherwise be impossible to play. The process is easy to understand, if one regards the *scordatura* as a musical change-over to summer or to winter time. The string players turn their peg, or pegs, up or down, generally a semitone. They then play the music *which is written for their fingers*, as if nothing had happened, and it will sound exactly as the composer wished it to. It is a perfectly simple affair—but conductors or players with perfect pitch hearing may feel seasick when looking at the printed music while it is being played.

Scordatura was frequently used in the 17th century, but also later, by Paganini, Spohr, Mahler, de Falla and others.

In the verbal communication between conductor and player referring to transposition, the conductor speaks of 'concert' (e.g. concert G) when he wishes to indicate the *pitch* of the sounds. If he refers to the score he calls it written G.

The score is the sum of the parts and the parts are written for the players: horn and trumpet players do not need key signatures in their parts, and traditionally rely on accidentals. This complicates the score's aspect even further.

When he looks at the score of a classical symphonic work, e.g. the first page of the first movement of Beethoven's Ninth Symphony, the conductor has therefore to face the following position:

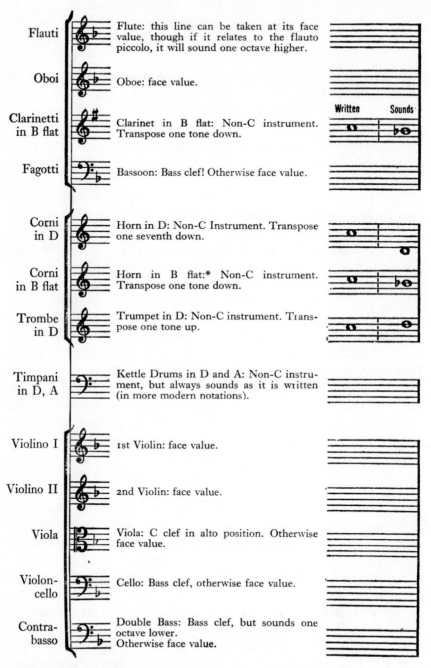

Flauti — Flute: this line can be taken at its face value, though if it relates to the flauto piccolo, it will sound one octave higher.

Oboi — Oboe: face value.

Written   Sounds

Clarinetti in B flat — Clarinet in B flat: Non-C instrument. Transpose one tone down.

Fagotti — Bassoon: Bass clef! Otherwise face value.

Corni in D — Horn in D: Non-C Instrument. Transpose one seventh down.

Corni in B flat — Horn in B flat:* Non-C instrument. Transpose one tone down.

Trombe in D — Trumpet in D: Non-C instrument. Transpose one tone up.

Timpani in D, A — Kettle Drums in D and A: Non-C instrument, but always sounds as it is written (in more modern notations).

Violino I — 1st Violin: face value.

Violino II — 2nd Violin: face value.

Viola — Viola: C clef in alto position. Otherwise face value.

Violoncello — Cello: Bass clef, otherwise face value.

Contrabasso — Double Bass: Bass clef, but sounds one octave lower. Otherwise face value.

---

* The Horn in B flat in Beethoven's Ninth Symphony is actually a Corno basso, and the transposition interval should therefore be a ninth.

The symphony orchestra referred to above constitutes for present circumstances a rather simple and straightforward arrangement. Nevertheless, the Shaw overture assumes a rather forbidding appearance as the result of the necessary adjustment for the different keys as well as for the transpositions.

			L				F				R̄					M			M			P	C
I		B				B		A	S	O	H			H		H	E	I			O		O	O
		F						J	Q				J		J		J	N	M		B	S		M	O
		G						L						Z		A			Z				I	S

		P				H		H	B				Z			C			S	V			H	J	H		A
J	O		P	B		S		S			G					J			J	G		E	O	I	O		J
	M					Z		D		H				F		B		O		N			G	K	C	B	C		S

	T			T									T			T				T												T	U

			I		O		I	B	W			I			I	R	H	H		O		I	H	N		M		I		R		I	T
		N		K		F	B	A				N			S	O	T	A		R		R	I	S		O		T		C		C	I
		O															Z			H		E				N	H	H		H		A	O
		G					A	S									Z		P	S	E		S	S		E		E		E		E	Z
	S				S		S					E					G			S	S					Y	S	S		S			S

The letters representing instruments in bass clef are lying on their right side; letters representing the instrumental alto clef (viola) are lying on their left. The alphabetical transpositions are made according to the following chart:

KEY TO TRANSPOSITION

	Clarine and Horn in B	Horn in D	Trumpet in D
A	B	H	Z
B	C	I	A
C	D	J	B
D	E	K	C
E	F	L	D
F	G	M	E
G	H	N	F
H	I	O	G
I	J	P	H
J	K	Q	I
K	L	R	J
L	M	S	K
M	N	T	L
N	O	U	M
O	P	V	N
P	Q	W	O
Q	R	X	P
R	S	Y	Q
S	T	Z	R
T	U	A	S
U	V	B	T
V	W	C	U
W	X	D	V
X	Y	E	W
Y	Z	F	X
Z	A	G	Y

The passage from *Androcles and the Lion* reads as follows: . . . . it is beginning to look as if Barabbas was a failure, in spite of his strong right hand, his victories, his empires, his millions of money, and his moralities and churches and political constitutions.

THIRD CHAPTER

THE ORCHESTRA
AND THE INSTRUMENTALIST

THE ORCHESTRA
AND THE INSTRUMENTALIST

It is the result of the discoveries that matters, not their intention: Columbus did not set out to discover America. In the late 16th century, a circle of friends around Count Bardi, the Florentine 'Camerata', got together in order to revive Greek tragedy with its accompanying music. They failed to realize their ambition, and unwittingly invented opera instead. Some technical terms, however, have remained and reflect their original intention, and one of these terms is the 'orchestra'.

In the theatres of ancient Greece, the orchestra was the space between the stage and the auditorium, the space in which the chorus and the instrumentalists moved. For the performances of the Camerata, the instruments were, to begin with, placed behind the scenery, but later they were moved to the front of the stage, i.e. to the space which corresponds to the Greek orchestra. This space, as well as the body of men within it, came to be called the orchestra.* Similarly, and interestingly enough, the Italian as well as the German word for chapel (cappella and Kapelle)† refer not only to the place itself, but also to the musicians who perform there. The transition from the ancient theatre to the modern opera house is shown by the Teatro Mimpico of Vicaaza.

Music probably began with percussion instruments only. It seems likely that the first orchestral effects were obtained in Egypt, Persia and Phoenicia by combining the sounds of harps, lyres, flutes, cymbals and drums, either in unison or in octaves.

---

* In America, this term comprises the main floor of the theatre as well.
† The German word for regimental band is 'Militärkapelle'.

The Greeks did not care for the orchestral effects of their neighbours, and cultivated mainly cytharas and lyres. Later, the Romans became masters in the construction and use of wind instruments, and every one of our modern wind instruments possesses a prototype among the wind instruments of the Roman Empire.

Concerted musical efforts before A.D. 1000 did not require scoring. Music was written as 'music per se', and not scored for individual instruments: not even the division of strings from wind instruments seemed necessary.

The earliest instrumental compositions date from the 15th century. Musical notation not only developed late, but its knowledge remained for a considerable period restricted to the monks and the troubadours: both of them were groups of people primarily concerned with *vocal* music. This fact led to the early notation of *vocal* music, whereas *instrumental* music, such as it was, was not recorded at all.

The independent existence of the orchestra we owe mainly to Monteverdi and Cavalli. The supremacy of the stringed instruments, too, was established by Monteverdi, who banished from the orchestra all those stringed instruments which are *not* played by bow, with the exception of the harp. Monteverdi's famous law: 'The preponderance of strings is essential for the balance of orchestral sound,' is as valid today as when it was first promulgated.

All stringed instruments which are played by bow are derived from the medieval viols. These were instruments which existed in various sizes, in order to suit the required pitch. The two main groups were the big ones, *viole da gamba*, which had to be steadied by the player's legs, and smaller ones, *viole da braccio*, which could be held with the arm. Gradually the stringed instruments as we know them were developed from these examples. In many public art collections the Renaissance paintings, as well as those of the Flemish, Dutch and German schools, reveal the variety of viols which once were in existence.

The development of the orchestra into the orchestra we now

know, became possible through the great advances in the technique of playing stringed instruments which resulted from the efforts of Jean Baptiste Lully, chief musician and composer to Louis XIV. As Giovanni Battista Lulli, a kitchen boy from Florence, he had emigrated to France in search of work; he died, 55 years old, in Paris in 1687. With the foundation of a new bow technique and an entirely new system of discipline, Lully led the first modern string orchestra, the *vingt-quatre violons du Roi*, to deserved fame. Later, he selected a group of sixteen *petits violons* and established a tradition of string playing which set an example to the rest of the world.

During the period of the continuo bass it was generally a single batch of violins which played opposite to the bass. Lully established our present five-tiered system of strings, i.e. first and second violins, violas, cellos and basses. Initially, the two bass instruments not only always played together, but even used the same written part, though the double bass, the *violone*, sounded one octave lower; the name violoncello is a diminutive of *violone*, and means the 'little double bass'.

The first wind instrument to join the strings was the oboe; it was followed by the bassoon.* This, with trumpets and drums for special occasions, completed the type of orchestra Händel wrote his music for. In Bach's Brandenburg Concerti, which are essentially *Concerti grossi*, the *Tutti* passages are mostly played by the strings only, and are counterpoised by varying solo instruments.

The middle of the 18th century saw a further important step in the progress of orchestral music. The town of Mannheim possessed at that time an excellent municipal orchestra, and supported gifted musicians. This attracted to the town the Czech-born musician J. Stamitz (1717-1757), who became the founder of the Mannheim School, a school to which we owe the development of orchestral dynamics with the introduction of the orchestral crescendo, and the introduction of the Minuet

---

* A computerized bassoon has recently been constructed.

as a third movement. Historically, this school occupies a position of transition between the concerto grosso orchestra and the classical symphony orchestra. Horns as well as clarinets had joined the orchestra, and it is reported that Mozart was filled with enthusiasm when he heard them play and that their orchestral sound influenced him considerably.

Under the influence of the previously undreamed-of technical accomplishments of the violin virtuosos, the first decades of the 19th century saw the great 'violin revolution'. Every violin up and down every country of the world had its neck broken. This was done in order to allow the pitch to be raised, an operation which in turn meant an increase in the tension of the strings, and consequential changes in the strings, the bow and the sound-board. The new necks were slightly longer (increased by one-quarter of an inch to the new measurement of seven and one-eighth inches) and were set back and strutted at a different, less flat angle: they permitted a new and superior technique. Nevertheless, it is from an artistic point of view regrettable that the violins of the famous Cremona masters, as well as all the other old master instruments—all wood-carvings of exquisite workmanship and great artistic merit—have now all become 'part-replaced antiques'.

The disappearance of the continuo after the period of the figured bass necessitated, in the interest of balancing the sound, not only the inclusion of new instruments, but also range and quality extensions of the existing ones. The flutes and other instruments which were new to the orchestra, rapidly extended their ranges upwards and downwards. The clarino was a high trumpet which Bach still used as a melody-carrying instrument: in Germany it was given the charming name of *Engelstrompete*, the 'angels trumpet', on account of the similarity of its shape with the shape of those trumpets which the angels traditionally blow in old paintings. It was a very difficult instrument to blow. Its rather handier successor, the clarinet (a diminutive of the clarino), introduced a new quality of sound. The horn, one of the oldest instruments—originally always a true ox's or ram's horn—became in its metal form the hunting field's contribution to the orchestra, and gave the sound picture a new type of support which led to its use as the orchestra's 'pedal'. Soon the classical orchestra became established and consisted of strings, 2 flutes, 2 oboes, 2 clarinets, 2 bassoons, 2-4 horns, 2 trumpets and, as a percussion instrument, the kettle drum only. In opera, and later also for symphonic music, 3 trombones were added.

In this pattern of scoring the classical orchestra became so successfully stabilized that composers returned again and again to its distribution of instruments, which seemed to produce a near-perfect mixture of sound qualities.

Haydn became the founder of modern orchestral usage by scoring for the orchestra's instruments in well-defined groups. He treated the orchestra as an independent power, opposed by solo instruments and by chorus. It is, however, interesting to recall that the greatest innovator of music, Austrian by origin, regarded himself as a link in the chain of a purely Italian tradition. If the conception of *Werktreue* (see p. 18) would extend to the composer's name as well, no work by Joseph Haydn would ever be performed: Haydn wished to be known as *Giuseppe Haydn*, and almost invariably signed his name in this form.

Beethoven emphasized the individuality of the different instruments by the solo passages he wrote for them. Schubert used the interplay of wood-wind in a new and ingenious manner. Weber gave new prominence to the horn and the clarinet.

The Romantic period delighted in conferring personal qualities to the instruments of the orchestra, an obvious trend which had already been in evidence in the programmatic music* of the 18th century. The viola was used to create an atmosphere of pensive melancholy. The oboe became identified with a maiden's or love's wistful sadness, the clarinet with sincerity, the trumpet with worldly power, and the trombone with heavenly power. The horn often represented the forest.

---

* Marin Marais (1656-1728), a Lully follower, even set to music an operation for the removal of gall-stones.

This new orchestral language, and the new suggestions of
'instrumental significance' were enriched by the discovery of a
new phenomenon, the phenomenon of the 'contrary effect'. It
was found that many musical instruments can, under certain
conditions, be used to express the opposite of their original and
accepted sentiment. The trumpet, for instance, the instrument
of the heroic and the majestic, can also sound oversentimental
and ludicrous, an effect used in the so-called 'laughing records,'
of the 1920s and 1930s. The flute, which in its higher regions
sounds as jubilant as the song of birds, sounds frightening and
awe-inspiring at the opposite end of its range. Weber has used
this effect with such skill that the low-lying thirds of the flutes
in the Wolf's Glen scene still send a shudder of ghostly fear
through *Freischütz* audiences.

The heavenly power of the trombones is expressed in their
forte: in piano, these instruments sound mysterious, admonitory
and awe-inspiring. The violins, superbly equipped to express
melodic cantability, become the devil's tool if their open fifths
are used as Tartini has used them in his famous *Devil's Trill
Sonata*, and in many other 'devilish' violin pieces. Stravinsky
found that the horn, which normally sounds strong and masculine, can assume a pathetic quality, as if a child was crying
for help, and has used this sound in an original way in *Petrushka*:
it was only necessary to insert a grace note in a way which, under
other conditions, might sound like the feared 'crack' or 'ghix',
in order to obtain this effect. Another unusual horn effect has
been successfully used by Benjamin Britten in his Serenade for
Tenor, Horn and Strings.

To this catalogue of contrary effects, the organ can as a
comparatively recent development be added as well. This old
instrument, which for hundreds of years has expressed the
exalted power of the Churches, underwent a few minor changes

—and became as the electronic organ a favourite mouthpiece for the trivial in music.

At the same time as this new interest in the characteristic timbre, the 'meaningful sound', arose a desire for an enlargement of the orchestra. Berlioz contemplated, and in his Requiem even accomplished, the orchestra of the thousand. Wagner augmented the orchestra by four tubas and a bass trumpet, which were especially constructed to his specifications. The representative numbers of the individual instruments, too, increased. Three, and even four, instead of two wind instruments were used, and enabled the individual wind instrument groups to give a three-chord effect. The piccolo flute extended the flute's range another octave upwards. The oboe acquired in the English horn a dark-sounding companion instrument.

The name of this latter instrument is a frequent source of confusion, and its derivation is of interest. The English horn is not a horn in the present meaning of the term; it belongs to the oboe family. The modern oboe is of French design, and already played important parts in Lully's orchestra. Its name comes from *haut bois*, the high woodwind, as opposed to the low woodwind or *basson*.

Many types of oboe existed. The name of the love-oboe, or oboe d'amore is due to its *coperchio (or piede) d'amore*, its 'love belly', a pear-shaped protrusion at the lower end. It was an A instrument, well-liked by Bach. Tuned in F, and called *oboe da caccia* (hunting oboe), the same instrument was, particularly in England, used for hunting. The English horn is the hunting oboe's refined and perfected version. If, therefore, a *horn* is defined as a wind-instrument which the mounted huntsman sounds to alert his hounds, then the English horn is—or was originally—a horn, and its name ceases to be a puzzle. The curved mouthpiece may stem from this primary use, as a long straight instrument is awkward to handle on horseback. Its lamenting and at the same time rather penetrating sound is very effectively used in Rossini's *William Tell* and in Wagner's *Tristan and Isolde*.

The clarinets, too, extended their influence. The third clarinet player became expected to blow bass clarinet as well, and Strauss' *Elektra* requires eight instruments of the clarinet family. Three trumpets, and sometimes four, began blowing together. The bass tuba offered a downwards extension to the brass.

The bassoon, an instrument which in its higher regions and in its staccato often acts as the light relief or the comedian of the orchestra, can sing with expression and beauty in its middle register. Wagner has used the bassoon to signify meanness (Beckmesser) or smallness (Alberich). It now found a downward extension (a whole octave lower) in the double-bassoon, which became one of the lowest instruments of the orchestra and supplied the wood-wind with dusky and mournful shading. Never has the double-bassoon been more movingly used than in the dungeon scene of *Fidelio* although Beethoven by the time he wrote this passage was hardly able to hear any of the sounds this instrument can produce.* In the first bars of *Le Sacre du Printemps* Stravinsky, too, has used this instrument very expressively.

Towards the turn of the century, the enlargement of orchestral power became more and more noticeable, though Berlioz's achievement in orchestral strength was never surpassed. Richard Strauss used 130 musicians for the *Alpen Symphonie*. Schönberg had for his *Gurre-Lieder*† special 48-line notepaper printed.

The opto-acoustic discrepancy, a result of the laws of physics and of the relative speed of sound, had by now suggested limitations of the size of the orchestra (see p. 83). The idea that

---

* Beethoven's deafness was of a 'conductive' type, in which the hearing for low sounds fails first. He was suffering from Ankylosis of the stapes (Otosclerosis).

† The *Gurre-Lieder* set the German translation of poems by the Danish writer Jens Peter Jacobsen (1847-85) to music. In Danish, *Gurre* is the name of a place, in German it signifies a decrepit horse.

intensification of sound must lead to its enrichment proved erroneous as well. A new sound phenomenon manifested itself, the 'sound cancellation' which meant that certain sound qualities can blot one another out. All this made the classical orchestra's composition appear desirable again, and revived interest in orchestral combinations of the past. Richard Strauss used a typical baroque combination of instruments for *Ariadne*, though he varied it by treating every single instrument as a solo instrument. Under the new name of 'chamber orchestra', the baroque orchestra became fashionable again.

Under the influence of Strauss' scoring, brass instruments were given more elaborate solo passages to blow. Percussion, too, was used in a new way. In the classical orchestra, percussion was represented only by kettledrums: they alone, the sole adjustable members of the percussion family, were deemed worthy of admission to an orchestra of sounds. The other percussion instruments (drums, cymbals, triangles, etc.) were not adjustable and therefore, strictly speaking, produced noises* and not sounds.

In the second movement of the Ninth Symphony, Beethoven used the kettledrum in a revolutionary manner. The 'outlaw' instruments, the noise makers, were referred to as 'Turkish music', and Beethoven used them only to convey Viennese ideas of Turkishness. Bruckner is reported to have consulted a considerable number of his friends before deciding —or rather before daring—to write the famous cymbal-crash into the score of the Adagio of his Seventh Symphony. Later, the wheel turned full circle, and in the *Danse Sacrale* of *Le Sacre du Printemps*, Stravinsky used the orchestra as a percussion band, thus initiating a demand for the 'percussion orchestra'. German music historians came to regard this development as an atavistic return to the very beginnings of music which were based on percussion as the only means of musical expression.

---

* Noise is defined as a sound which contains many components which are *not* simple multiples of the fundamental.

In the 17th century, the King's twenty-four violins of Lully had represented the first orchestra of musical importance. To the musical interest of the Austrian aristocracy of the second half of the 18th century we owe, to a considerable extent, the symphony type of orchestra.

During the 19th century (in 1842) the New York Philharmonic Orchestra was founded, and in the same year the Vienna Philharmonic Orchestra emerged as a special section of the orchestra of Vienna' Imperial and Royal (K. und k.) Opera House, to rival Austria's other and more famous opera house, the Teatro alla Scala in Milan.

Later, the Berlin Philharmonic Orchestra came into prominence, largely because it came to be conducted by masters such as Bülow. Nikisch and Furtwängler.

The highly gifted German pianist Karl Halle (1819-95) was born in Hagen, a town which on account of its iron, steel and textile industries has been called 'Prussia's Manchester'. In 1836 he emigrated to Paris and became a friend of Liszt, Chopin and Berlioz. After the unrests of 1848 he moved to London, and in 1856, having changed his name to Charles Hallé, he eventually settled in Manchester. In 1857 he brought into being England's first orchestra in a symphonic sense—only orchestras serving the choral societies had existed before. It was followed by the Bournemouth Symphony Orchestra in 1893, and in 1905 by the London Symphony Orchestra. Sir Thomas Beecham (1879-1961) successively founded both the London Philharmonic Orchestra in 1932, and the Royal Philharmonic Orchestra in 1946.

The enormous rise in maintenance costs has made opera companies and orchestras dependent on subventions from public-spirited bodies and individuals — though it is certainly a matter of regret and concern that symphonic and operatic music are used in order to advertise cancer-producing habits. At the present time, the radio stations and the record companies have assumed the role of Maecenas as the patron of orchestras.

The orchestra's seating-order, too, underwent changes.

While the orchestra was conducted from the harpsichord, it seemed desirable to place the violins in the centre. With the disappearance of the harpsichord, different seating plans came to be adopted by different orchestras. In the French operatic tradition all strings were seated to the left, and all wind instruments to the right of the conductor. The classical symphony arrangement of central Europe placed the first violins to the left, and the second violins to the right of the conductor; later, it was claimed that this arrangement was unfavourable to the concord of the violins.

Two reasons were given in support of this contention: firstly, that the violin players cannot hear one another as well as when they are sitting side by side, and secondly, that their violins will sound differently, since the first violins tilt their instruments *towards* the public as it were, and the second violins tilt them *away* from it. This argument resulted in the tendency to place the second violins on the same side as, and behind, the first violins, and the celli and violas filled the space vacated by the second violins, on the conductor's right.

This arrangement, which originated in England, was introduced into the United States by Stokowski and is now, at least on the continent of Europe, referred to as the American arrangement. It is, however, never used by the New York Philharmonic Orchestra, because Arturo Toscanini, its famous conductor, was disinclined to adopt it. Recently the American arrangement has become widely accepted in Europe, though not the American practice of using raised benches in amphitheatrical fashion, a practice which is meant to make it easier to see the orchestra's work and to increase the sound individuality of the various instruments.

It is argued against this arrangement that it distorts visual symmetry. It is also claimed that the first and second violins are scored differently, and that the slight difference in sound-character which results from the different tilt of the instruments may well be a desirable rather than an undesirable one. It has a further disadvantage: everyone agrees that the double basses should be placed behind the celli, though it is not necessary that they should be placed *directly* behind the celli. In their traditional position, the celli face the conductor; this makes it possible to place the double basses at the very back, facing the audience, which is probably their most effective position. If the celli occupy the place which the second violins occupy by tradition, i.e. on the right hand of the conductor, the new position forces the basses—possibly to the detriment of the orchestral sound—to the extreme right.

The argument about the placing of the instruments became at one stage rather heated and the controversy became further complicated by arguments of visual and aural balance. Sir Adrian Boult* expressed his views with characteristic forcefulness:

". . . it has, sadly, now become the practice to let the strings radiate round the conductor in the order of firsts, second violins on the firsts' left, violas next more or less in the middle, and 'cellos on the right, with basses behind them. I would advise even the least inexperienced forces against this practice. It is a little easier for the performers in some ways perhaps, but surely the principal thing is that the audience should get a balanced aural picture (visual also if that matters), and so I always place the second violins on my right, so that they balance the firsts, and in the same way I like to have my 'cellos towards the middle of the stage, and the basses also in the middle but further back of course; perhaps even behind the woodwind who are usually grouped in the middle behind the strings, with brass divided each side of the woodwind group."

The seating arrangements do not matter as much as many people believe; tradition and personal predilections influence the various opinions professed far too strongly. Splendid performances are possible with either of the two, as well as with some other seating arrangements, and there exist very few rules which are not meant to be infringed. There are really only four such rules:

---

* Sir Adrian Boult, *A Handbook on the Technique of Conducting* (London, 1968), p.25.

1. The first violins should be on the left of the conductor (except at Bayreuth, where on account of the orchestra's cowl, the sound of the first violins improves if they are 'tilted away' and they therefore sit on the conductor's right hand).

2. The trumpets and trombones must be seated so that they blow across the stage and not into the faces of the audience. (This rule, too, has on occasions been most successfully broken.)

3. The *leading* instruments in the wood-wind group should be in the centre, and the second and third instruments should spread outwards from the firsts.

4. The double basses must be behind the celli (though not necessarily directly behind them), because they underline, often directly, the celli from an octave below.

The orchestra represents an extraordinary conglomeration of men and machines. The present operatic orchestra is a body of about 100 men, and if it were a democratic assembly, the strings would always govern it, because they (i.e. the first and second violins, violas, celli and basses), form, in accordance with Monteverdi's law, a majority of at least 60 out of 100.

This majority does not give the strings any special rights: not even the right to fix the pitch they want for their 'A'. The 'A' to which the orchestra is tuned is traditionally supplied by the oboe, though whenever a 'fixed tone' instrument (piano or harpsichord) is used in the orchestra, everyone has to tune from this instrument, which in turn was tuned a short time before the performance from a tuning-fork.

The strings' prerogative is that they supply the 'leader of the orchestra', which exalted title refers to the man playing the first violin on the outside (the public's side) of the first violin desk, to the left hand of the conductor. His position is really an anachronism, a relic from the days before conductors. Prior

to the introduction of the conductor in the modern sense—
really a 19th century innovation—the direction of the music was
vested in the 'maestro di concerto', the violinist leader of the
orchestra. As director of the orchestra, he was in due course
replaced by the 'maestro al cembalo', i.e. the conductor who was
seated at the harpsichord.

Apart from playing the solo violin passages, the leader of
the orchestra has nowadays no special musical function in an
orchestra, though he still enjoys the traditional right of immediate access to the conductor as the spokesman for his
orchestra. It is also customary for the leader, or the 'concert
master' to take his seat later than the rest of the members of the
orchestra and, particularly in the concert hall, to take his own
'curtain call'. This is a—possibly unjustified—survival from the
past, and its use is restricted to England. Actually, another
member of the orchestra might now be more entitled to be
singled out for applause: the union's representative, on account
of his having to give permission to extend the rehearsal time.
He may well belong to the wind section.

The qualifications, the education and the professional status
of the members of an orchestra are generally very similar. All
members of an orchestra have gone through their 'seven hours
a day for seven years' stint to master the basic technique of
their instrument. Most have spent three or four years at a music
academy or conservatory. Many can play several instruments.
Most viola players have played the violin,* and members of
the wind section often play more than one wood-wind or brass
instrument.

All players share, or *did* share a sincere and deep-seated
love of music. Yet, an exasperated conductor once defined an
orchestra as a group of men 'half of whom do not want to be

---

* It is commonly assumed that violin players must have fine, delicate fingers,
and that those whose fingers are rather large change over to the viola. This is
quite untrue: practically all violin players have fingers of the shape and size
one would expect in a farmer or butcher.

there, while the other half have no business to be there'.

It is a well-known fact that orchestral playing can become a dead-end job. The string players, the violinists and cellists in particular, did in most cases set out on their career with the intention—or hope—of becoming virtuoso soloists. To play in an orchestra can be an excellent temporary experience, but the prospect of spending year after year in the pit, 'at the dirty end of the stick', is frustrating for a would-be soloist: it is the manifestation of an ambition which went wrong, and of a hope disappointed. A great many violin players may well feel that they would have never chosen this career had they known from the beginning that they would be unable to rise above orchestral musicianship. Of course, all professions are full of people who have aimed at loftier targets than they were actually able to achieve, but in music failure tastes even more bitter than elsewhere. The difference in status and modus vivendi between a successful soloist and an orchestral fiddler is enormous, even if the actual difference in accomplishment is, at times, quite surprisingly small.

The members of the chorus of the opera houses represent in some respects the vocal equivalent of the orchestra. Every opera house needs a large permanent, and an even larger facultative, chorus. The permanent requirement, totalling eighty or so singers, comprises about twenty singers for each of four vocal groups, i.e. soprano, contralto, tenor and bass (basses and baritones are lumped together). Each member of the chorus must be an accomplished artist, and the would-be entrant has to go through gruelling auditions before he or she is accepted. For many young singers chorus work is a good experience, but as a career it is beset by similar troubles to those mentioned above: almost always the chorister is a would-be soloist, and chorus work can eventually become unsatisfactory and frustrating. However—and the same applies to string players—in middle age, after the passionate years of youthful ambitions have passed, it can fortunately come to a happy and resigned acceptance of one's limitations. In their newly-found contentment and long experience, such artists form the most valuable core of chorus and orchestra.

Orchestral playing is not always very remunerative, and it is not surprising that competent instrumentalists will eventually leave a good orchestra if a substantially higher-paid vacancy, even if the work is musically less rewarding, offers itself elsewhere. This drift causes vacancies which have often to be filled by young people who have just completed their preparatory studies. These, strictly speaking, should not be there, or rather, should not *yet* be there, as symphonic playing in a good orchestra is a difficult task and requires years of experience in orchestral team-work. This experience can only be obtained in the proper way if the 'young entry' is kept in manageable proportions to the experienced members of the team.

The old saying that 'love makes the time pass, but time makes love pass' applies to the love of music as well. A life of rather dreary rehearsals, a life of work with uninspiring conductors, and all this in the general setting of a rather limited prosperity in comparison with other professions, does not always stimulate the production of the exuberant sound of perfectly played music. In this aspect, too, the personality of the conductor is of greatest importance. The genius of a masterly conductor can inspire even the most disillusioned orchestra-hack, and renew his dormant love for music-making. As bored by their circumstances, and as disappointed by the absence of personal success as they may be, few orchestral musicians will fail to respond to a great leader.

Fortunate indeed is the conductor who can revivify his orchestra's latent enthusiasm. He must be a good psychologist. He must be able to coax, to praise and to reprimand in the required doses, well aware that the relationship between orchestra and conductor, in spite of the players' ages, is apt to make a schoolroom atmosphere return. It is surprising how easily grown-up men can revert to schoolboy pranks; such pranks are facilitated by the fact that the conductor can generally see his players only from the nose upwards: the rest is hidden by the music stand.

The players can see rather more of him when they do look, down to his chest in fact,* but they can only look at him at certain moments, as they must also look at the music in front of them. (The best way to observe the optic link between player and conductor is to look from the front-row seat of an opera theatre into the eye of a player directly opposite. The movement of his eyes towards the conductor will be obvious. On account of the seating arrangements, it will be generally a viola- or cello-player whose eyes can be followed most readily.)

The conductor who knows how to make an initially critical crowd of players respect and admire him, will eventually emerge as their hero. The conductor is generally well aware that he sets out from a position of disadvantage; he is, to some extent, always the 'natural enemy' of his orchestra and to achieve full acceptance is not an easy task.

Exactly how he sets about it is up to him. All ways are good if they are successful. The salient point is that the individual players must recognize him as a master-musician. The path to his acceptance can be tricky and beset with pitfalls. Some members of the orchestra may—particularly if he has in their view been a little opinionated—feel inclined to 'find him out'. This can lead to a situation where he may sustain serious or even irrecoverable loss of face and authority if he does fall into the trap laid for him. Such traps can be quite elaborate, though, in an attitude of fair play for the audience, they are generally only laid at rehearsals. At the beginning of the third act of *Tosca*, for instance, is a passage which four horns blow in unison. If the horn players conspire to blow this phrase a semitone too low, the subsequent entry of the basses at the correct pitch

---

* A different perspective applies in theatres with a deep orchestra pit, in which the conductor's place is raised for the benefit of the singers.

will throw the sound into utter confusion.* Of course, the
conductor should notice the incorrect pitch at once, and with
the stop-signal of the baton, a double knock, interrupt before
any confusion can arise. It is, however, a difficult and severe
test, and a well-known conductor was so shaken and dejected
when he failed to notice this trap that he felt unable to continue,
and had to leave the rehearsal.

If a conductor successfully passes such trials, respect for
him is assured. Whether he is subsequently polite, or at times
even rough, does not matter so much any more. It is his job to
correct, and it is his right to request improvements. As long
as his demands impress the players as justified, and their results
appear desirable, correction is readily accepted, and even
occasional sarcasm is tolerated. If the conductor is entitled to
have highly competent musicians at his command, he is also
entitled to expect from them masterly handling of their instruments. He must, of course, hear any imperfection at once and
insist on appropriate rectification. A well justified criticism is
allowed to contain its sting.

Only two instrumentalists must be treated with kid gloves:
no conductor likes to rebuke the horn-player or the oboist.
These two instruments carry their own unforeseeable risks, and
things can go wrong even if they are played by true masters.
As the result of an 'act of God', and in spite of flawless technique,
sudden muscle-tiredness can make the horn crack, and the oboe
can go wrong as the result of an unaccountable loss of muscular
tension in the masseter-muscle of the cheek. That it is tiredness
which produces such mishaps is so well recognized that few
orchestras will let their horn-players blow throughout a long
work. In long Wagner operas, e.g. *Die Meistersinger von Nürnberg*,
the horns generally only blow for half of the performance, and

---

* The first bars of the overture to *Oberon*, too, can be used for such mischief—
  though, as this passage is played by a single horn, the insubordination involved carries greater personal risk.

a second team of horn players must be ready to take over where the first team leaves off.

The double reeds too pose a special problem. In the orchestral noise before the performance, oboe and bassoon sounds are often conspicuous, and their players can be seen to bite and chew on their reeds. The hazards of these instruments are so well recognized that considerate composers have inserted special 'warming up notes' for them which are quite unnecessary for the orchestral sound. In *Carmen*, for instance, a note of this type just before the 'Flower Aria' gives the English horn player the opportunity to warm up and prepare for his famous solo passage—particularly as his instrument has not yet been used during the opera.

The need to play in front of the microphone has substantially improved the technical aspect of music making, though it may well be that the need for flawless technical perfection has led to an exaggeration of the technical aspects of music at the expense of its spiritual values.

Little mishaps (grave mistakes are in orchestral language referred to as a 'Domino') occur even in the best orchestras. Such mishaps used to be dreaded occurrences; perhaps as a result of the gramophone recordings, our attitude to them has recently undergone a change. During recording-sessions even little mishaps are invariably eliminated by repetition of the passage, and subsequent insertion of the perfect version. This is a well justified practice, as in listening to the gramophone record the reiteration of a flaw would make it a very annoying feature. We are, however, now beginning to realize that such a degree of perfection can deaden a rendering. Everyone in the orchestra must aim at perfection, but little mishaps are human and they 'belong'. Absolute perfection is soulless, and unnatural.

FOURTH CHAPTER

THE PRODUCER

THE PRODUCER

The producer of an opera is much less restricted by tradition than is its conductor or singer. The conductor's art is governed by the rules of good music making. The singer is, by and large, subject to the rules of bel canto. For the producer, all's fair, just as it is in love and war: it is only the result which counts.

The need to 'produce' an opera is as old as opera itself. Indeed, the Camerata operas contained a surprising number of stage effects, ranging from fountains to a variety of manifestations of the *Deus ex machina*. One must assume that it was the duty of the composer to see to the technicalities of their production.

In England, opera production began with Henry Purcell (1659-1695), who was born 15 years after Monteverdi's death. His work is rich in items requiring 'staging'—perhaps due to the fact that he had progressed to the writing of opera by way of writing incidental stage music for a large number of dramatic works. Quite probably he, too, was personally responsible for the smooth working of his stage effects.

It is well known that Mozart took an active interest in production aspects, particularly those of his later works.

Towards the middle of the 19th century, production was generally limited to the strict execution of the directions contained in the score, and the necessary supervision and direction was in most cases entrusted to emeritus singers.

Before the modern producer came into his own, the painters of the back-drop and the wings were in many respects the most important people in the operatic production team. Those painters were artists of considerable merit, and their name was generally given on the programme. At that time, three-dimensional decorations did not exist on the stage, and this made the painter's work much more important than it is now. Later on, the use of three-dimensional decorations led to a revolutionary change in stage construction and stage dimensions, but this happened only after the introduction of electric lighting into the opera houses, i.e. about the time of *Aida*. The artistic merit of the early back-drop paintings explains the current search for the old, often charmingly painted original canvasses, and the keen desire—particularly in Italy—to make use of them whereever this is feasible.

Verdi and Wagner, the two divergent geniuses of that operatic vintage year 1813, behaved in respect of production with characteristic difference. Verdi did not wish to know anything about the creative producer; all he demanded was strict adherence to the given directions. Wagner, on the other hand, became so absorbed in the possibilities of production that in order to be able to devote himself in his own theatre at Bayreuth completely to the needs of production, he repeatedly opted to forgo conducting.

Gustav Mahler, who is really the founder of modern operatic producing was the first director of an opera house to insist on purposeful and meaningful production. His views on the need for convincing production of opera gave the Vienna Opera House during his directorship its distinctive style.

The modern producer's basic task is to choose the setting for the interpretation, a task which necessitates the help of a designer, as well as of other ancillary services. He then has to proceed to develop the expression of his own interpretation through the singers. This involves not only the control of their stage movements, but also of their facial expressions and—particularly in operas which include spoken dialogue (e.g. *Entführung aus dem Serail, Carmen, Fidelio*, etc.)—even certain detailed oral inflections.

The great ambition of the operatic producer is to create

and direct the perfect actor-singer or singer-actor. This is an ambition which can be realized only under the most exceptional circumstances. Its difficulty is due to the fact that in opera all emotion arises from the score, and all production has to spring directly out of the music. This explains too why conductors often feel that they themselves make the best producers, and why conductors have frequently excelled in this field. In fact, many conductors reluctant to undertake the double task of conducting and producing, regard themselves nevertheless as the real producers, and only delegate, as it were, some aspects of their work to the professional producer. The relationship between conductor and producer is therefore one which is always fraught with the risk of friction, and if during rehearsals a producer is heard to say to the conductor: 'May we have this a little slower (or faster), please?' ignition can be expected.

Some conductors prefer to give the producer a completely free hand, and this freedom has led to the comparatively recent appearance of the highly skilled, and often highly successful, independent producer. This became a trend which led to many notable achievements, among them some remarkable productions of Mozart Operas during the Busch and Ebert period at Glyndebourne.

Wieland Wagner's work in Bayreuth proved of particular significance. Essentially a specialized effort, it nevertheless assumed such general importance that it has influenced the production of opera everywhere to a quite unexpected degree. Its main innovation consisted in discarding the old, worn-out ornamental stage items, and their replacement, on an all but bare stage, by the significance as well as the tremendous impression-potential of meaningful single and group movements.

The present trend for specialization in producing is gathering momentum, and 'Richard Strauss production specialists', as well as specialists in the operatic application of the principles of the *commedia dell'arte* have come to the fore in Germany and Italy. Some of the 'general' producers, too, have deservedly made great names for themselves, and it is not surprising to find among them some whose musical knowledge and practical musicianship is almost as high as that of a conductor. In some cases the producer may well be a *Maestro manqué*. In other instances, active singers as well as ex-star-performers of the operatic world have tried their hand at producing, and have shown that their special experience can be put to very good use in this field.

The difficulties which confront the modern producer are considerable. During the last 60 or 70 years, many attempts have been made to adapt the style of operatic production to the changing artistic movements of the day: to Impressionism, to Expressionism, to New Realism, etc. In this respect, production encounters certain difficulties and problems of its own, problems which the music does not need to face: to separate a production's style from the fashions set by its own period is proving notoriously difficult.

The producer has a number of stylistic approaches open to him.

He can:

1. produce opera in a style characteristic of the period of the opera's creation;

2. produce opera in a style relating to the period of the opera's action;

3. produce opera in a style which at the time of the opera's creation was regarded as appropriate for the period of the opera's action. This method could be called the method of 'charming anachronism' and its trump-card lies in the fact that pictorial art has used it with great success. It received its accolade by the painters of the 16th and 17th centuries, who habitually painted Romans and Greeks as well as mythological or biblical personages according to their own, contemporary views as to how these people might have dressed, acted and lived. Strictly speaking, the results are anachronisms as they reflect to a large extent 16th and 17th century customs. Nevertheless, we

find this method charming as well as appropriate, and it has been successfully accepted for many operatic productions;

4. produce opera as though it was written more recently than in fact it was (i.e. bring it forward), or

5. produce opera in a fantastic or fairy-tale type of setting.

The present attitude to producing is liberal, and favours boldness and unorthodoxy. Attempts to solve age-old production problems by a new 'no holds barred' approach are encouraged. It has, for example, been suggested that the notorious difficulty of the last act of Puccini's *Manon Lescaut* might be resolved by making it a prologue to the opera, with the other acts produced on the 'flash back' principle. Such ideas are interesting, but they produce musical difficulties, and it remains doubtful how the public will react to such transplant surgery. Certain experiments with unorthodox means of operatic presentation have been unexpectedly successful, e.g. the production of *The Damnation of Faust* at the London Coliseum.

The qualities which we expect from a producer make a formidable list: knowledge of music, unimpeachable good taste, an eye for the theatrically effective, some knowledge of the history of art, and, on top of all this, a gift for applied psychology. The producer should also be able to express himself adequately in operatic languages or, at least have helpful friends who are prepared to assist him with his language problems.

The reciprocal expectations which exist between the producer and the other members of the operatic team, and the public, can be summarized as follows:

THE SINGER EXPECTS FROM THE PRODUCER:

1. *Perfect command of the 'geography' of the role and full understanding of its context and social background.*

2. *The discipline of being prepared to listen to the singer's*

ideas, and willingness to adapt his own ideas to those of the singer wherever this seems reasonable.

3. *The realization that the singer, although he is an actor who carries his instrument around with him, nevertheless needs a place to stand it on. He must not be expected to sing while hanging by one arm over an abyss, however effective it might be theatrically.*

4. *Realization that physical aptitude, deportment and agility vary enormously from one person to another, even if they can sing the same role.*

5. *A singer must feel that he can have absolute confidence in the producer's 'house eye'. This means that if a producer assures him that a dress, hat or action, which from the stage seems uncomely, nevertheless is good and effective when seen from the house, the singer must be able to accept this assurance with confidence.*

THE PRODUCER EXPECTS FROM THE SINGER:

1. *Wholehearted collaboration, i.e. absence of overt or hidden resistance, and an open mind. This implies the discarding of preconceived notions left over from past productions, and detachment from the recollection of the marvellous things which von Katerscheiss has done at Surmheim Opera House, or Menefreghi in the open air at Piede di Rasta.*

2. *The conscientious honouring of bona fide agreements, which means that the singer must not revert in front of the public to his own ideas, after he has ostensibly fulfilled the producer's wishes during the rehearsals.*

THE CONDUCTOR EXPECTS FROM THE PRODUCER:

The effective realization of those production ideas which he himself has always been dreaming about.

THE PRODUCER EXPECTS FROM THE CONDUCTOR:

> *To be left in peace.*

THE PRODUCER EXPECTS FROM THE PUBLIC:

> *Immediate recognition and enthusiastic reception of all the new ideas which he has incorporated into the production.*

THE PUBLIC EXPECTS FROM THE PRODUCER:

> *That he should not tamper with those production details, however corny they may be, which they have enjoyed during the last* 30 *years, and change those which they have not liked.*

The potential rewards for the capable producer are considerable. Only quite recently has the producer joined the principal singers and the conductor in taking the final curtain call, but this practice has no doubt come to stay. By his ability, the producer has made the public well aware of his work, and has opened up a new seam in the mine of artistic enterprise— with all the glory and the rewards it can bring to the famous and successful in this new art.

FIFTH CHAPTER

THE SOUND
AND THE SINGER

THE SOUND AND THE SINGER

To sing meant originally 'to resound': "We hear this fearful tempest sing."* Everyone can sing, but few people would care to listen to just anybody singing. In speaking, the human voice generally does not make an attractive sound. The sound of speech only becomes beautiful by its circumstances: it is a beautiful sound when it breaks loneliness or fear, or when it is the voice of someone we love and long for. Otherwise, only content and meaning account for the pleasantness of the spoken word. To be forced to listen to *spoken* words which one does not understand, is, on the whole, an unpleasant experience.

No fundamental difference of function divides speaking from singing, and for this reason medical science lumps the two activities together and simply calls it 'phonation'. The flow of speech is governed by word-accent and by the phrase- or sentence-accent, which adapts the rise and fall of the voice to the sense of the words. In singing, we use our faculty *deliberately* to impart variable vibration frequencies to our voice. In this way we consciously produce musical notes, though we execute the necessary muscular adjustment subconsciously.

Pitch and length of notes then take over as the significant feature, and word and phrase-accent become secondary. In between the two activities of singing and speaking stands the 'declamation'.

Provided the voice is reasonably pleasant, it is always

---

* Richard II, ll. i. 263.

enjoyable to listen to someone who sings. When true musical quality is added to the 'resounding', the result can be enchanting, and all the more so if the sound of the voice is really beautiful.

For opera a beautiful voice is not enough; the voice must also possess volume and must carry well, without losing its beauty in the process. It is surprising how little we know about the physiological mechanism of voice-production, and many claims of singing teachers in this respect are sheer humbug. The only facts we know for certain are that the voice is produced by the vibration of the vocal cords, and that the resulting sound is a 'mixed sound', which is amplified by the resonators of the pharynx, mouth, nose and chest. We have no idea what anatomical circumstances favour the development of a big voice, or what it is which in some cases gives a very soft voice special carrying power or beauty.

The beauty and the power of a singing voice are, alas, evanescent. They can fade without any noticeable sign of illness or disease, and as yet we cannot understand why this should be.

Every voice 'carries' to some extent, and we know fairly accurately what distances are within range of human vocal power: it is comparatively simple to measure experimentally the distance over which the sound of the human voice, in its various intensities, can be heard.

The softest voice is the so-called 'ideal whisper' which is the sound the human voice produces by using 'residual air' only. Residual air is the air which remains in our lungs *after* a full expiration: in order to produce an ideal whisper, we have to exhale completely and then whisper, before taking a fresh breath. The sound thus produced can, under perfect conditions (i.e. those of near perfect silence in a tree-lined avenue on a windless day), carry approximately 40 feet.

The 'accentuated' whisper voice or 'forced' whisper is produced by whispering with *full* breath, and words thus produced can under the same conditions be understood quite well at a distance of about 80 feet.

'Conversational' voice, i.e. our normal speaking voice, is subject to individual differences which are rather bigger in normal speaking than in whispering. Under suitable conditions, loudly spoken words can remain audible at a distance of about 300 feet.

Over-loud conversational voice (i.e. shouting, calling loudly or yelling), tested under similar conditions can be heard quite accurately up to about 800 feet.

Noisy conditions—even a very moderate noise—reduce all these distances drastically.

Most people's singing voice carries somewhat further than their speaking voice, but if an attempt is made to use the voice to communicate across greater distances it quickly degenerates into an ugly sound and becomes shouting or yelling. A singer's voice must carry at least as far as the 'yelling voice' of an ordinary mortal, and must not lose any of its beauty in the process. This can generally be neither learned nor acquired, and the great voice is therefore essentially a 'gift'.

The carrying power of the human voice loses its strength in direct proportion to the square of the distance from its place of origin, i.e. from the mouth (see p. 90). The vocal intensity which a singer must be able to emanate in order to be heard plainly at the diagonally opposite end of a theatre,* notwithstanding a considerable orchestral 'din', is quite remarkable, although the room acoustics are of great help.

Sound travels rather slowly. Its speed of 1120 feet per second (or $12\frac{1}{2}$ miles per minute), compares quite miserably with the speed of light, which proceeds at the rate of almost as many millions of miles per minute (11 000 000). This opto-acoustic discrepancy (see p. 56) proved to be the limiting factor in the use of the thousands of instruments and voices to which some 19th century composers aspired, and it came to impose a practical limit upon the size of orchestras and choirs. If we

---

* A distance of 150 feet or even more.

the very front row and the men in the very last row will see the
conductor's beat simultaneously, and, in correct response will
imagine a very large choir, it is perfectly clear that the ladies in
produce their sounds simultaneously. However, due to the
physical phenomenon of opto-acoustic discrepancy, the audience
will be aware of the time-lag which arises *in between* the sounds
of the front and those of the back, and therefore will *not* perceive
these sounds at the *same* time.

In the open, the sound waves radiate from their centre of
origin like the familiar ripples of the water disturbed by a stone.
This gives the sound a 'dead' quality, which for music is not
desirable, and which explains why music in the open is generally
not very satisfactory. However, its sound can be considerably improved if at least one wall (the 'orchestra shell') is erected behind
the orchestra.

Optimum room acoustics enhance the enjoyment derived
from listening to music, and the physical and architectural
sciences have lately made great progress towards the creating
of such conditions. Every wall which is struck by the ripple of
the sound waves causes a reflection of waves, and this manifests
itself in reverberation within the room. Each reflection will then
be re-reflected, and this brings not only an increase in intensity,
but also levels out the intensity as far as the whole room is concerned. Different structural materials have different 'sound
swallowing' and sound reflecting properties, and their judicious
use permits the creation of excellent acoustic conditions. It has
lately been found that the ideal resonance for all types of music
is one which lasts from 1 to $2\frac{1}{2}$ seconds. It is well within our
power, by suitable construction and the use of suitable reflecting
and damping materials, to adjust rooms to such tolerances.

The great progress in physical acoustics during the last
decades went hand in hand with a rapidly expanding voice-
preserving and voice-reproducing industry. This led to the
introduction of new acoustic measures, and we are now able
to measure voice, as well as noise intensities, accurately in new
units, the phon and the bel. These two units are closely related

to one another. Due to the fact that loudness varies greatly with vibration frequency, they involve highly complicated mathematical calculations.

Our hearing mechanism shows an extraordinary variation in its sensitivity to sounds. The musical scale is fixed by the pitch of the note A, for which from 1859-1939 the 'French concert pitch' was the accepted standard. This pitch was based on the A of a vibration frequency of 435 cycles per second. In 1939 an internationally accepted pitch was in London fixed at 440 cycles per second, which gave the 12-interval chromatic scale the frequencies shown on the next page.*

We can hear sounds from 16 to 20,000 cycles, though in the very low frequencies, particularly from 16 to 64 cycles, the sensation of vibration predominates over that of hearing. The ear can, therefore, be justly compared to a measuring instrument which can measure *miles* at one end of its range, while at the other end of it still able to detect changes of less than one-eighth of an inch. The musical range extends only up to approximately 3,500 cycles, which is the small flute's upper limit. Only the organ can cover the whole range from 16 to 4,186 cycles per second (C^{-3} to C^5). It is noteworthy that our ear is far more sensitive to sounds in the range of from 1,000 to 2,500 cycles, than to the sounds outside this range.†

Altogether, our ear can detect about 2,000 gradations in the pitch of sounds. Beyond a frequency of 20,000 cycles we cannot hear sounds at all, whatever their intensity may be. Dogs can hear such frequencies easily, and this faculty is made use of in the dog-whistle which produces sounds of approximately 20,000 cycles. This whistle remains silent to us, even though the sound which the dog hears is so loud that it makes him put his paws over his ears.

---

* This table, as well as the two tables on p. 127, are based on *Documenta Geigy Scientific Tables*, Basle, 1956.

† The physiological data of this section are based on Samson Wright, *Applied Physiology*, Oxford, 1966.

Vibration frequencies of the 12-interval chromatic scale

A = 440.0 cps

	C^{-3}	C^{-2}	C^{-1}	C^{0}	C^{1}	C^{2}	C^{3}	C^{4}
C	16.35	32.70	65.41	130.81	261.63	523.25	1046.50	2093.00
C *sharp* D *flat*	17.32	34.65	69.30	138.59	277.18	554.37	1108.73	2217.46
D	18.35	36.71	73.42	146.83	293.66	587.33	1174.66	2349.32
D *sharp* E *flat*	19.45	38.89	77.78	155.56	311.13	622.25	1244.55	2489.02
E	20.60	41.20	82.41	164.81	329.63	659.26	1318.51	2637.02
F	21.83	43.65	87.31	174.61	349.23	698.46	1396.91	2793.83
F *sharp* G *flat*	23.12	46.25	92.50	185.00	369.99	739.99	1479.98	2959.96
G	24.50	49.00	98.00	196.00	392.00	783.99	1567.98	3135.96
G *sharp* A *flat*	25.96	51.91	103.83	207.65	415.30	830.61	1661.22	3322.44
A	27.50	55.00	110.00	220.00	440.00	880.00	1760.00	3520.00
A *sharp* B *flat*	29.14	58.27	116.54	233.08	466.16	932.33	1864.66	3729.31
B	30.87	61.74	123.47	246.94	493.88	987.77	1975.53	3951.07

Physically, sound intensity is measured by the amount of vibratory energy which flows through the standard area of one square centimeter, placed at right angles to the direction of sound propagation, per unit of time. The variation in sound energy which is necessary between the softest sound we can possibly hear and the loudest noise we can just tolerate is simply enormous: the sound energy for the sound we can just tolerate without feeling pain, is one million times greater than that required for threshold hearing.

In view of the huge range of intensities involved, a scale of change in intensity (relative loudness, i.e. damping and amplification) has been evolved. Its unit is the bel, and if the intensity of a sound increases ten times, the intensity level is raised by one bel. It is therefore a logarithmic scale.

The decibel, which is one-tenth of a bel, is more convenient for practical use. The decibel is the smallest change in intensity which can be detected by the human ear. The sound energy required for it is about equal to that required in playing a 1,000 cycles per second note, so as to be just at the threshold of audibility for young people. In other words the decibel can be portrayed thus:

With the threshold of human hearing based at nought, the following table, which is a logarithmic one, gives selected samples of loudness. It also marks the threshold of pain caused by sound.

Decibel

Absolute silence   Auditory threshold .   .   0

Faint noise   Gentle breeze   10

Ticking of watch   Very quiet house .   .   20

Quiet garden   Ideal whisper .   .   .   30

Residential district without traffic .   .   40

General office noise   Accentuated whisper .   50

Ordinary conversation   Street traffic .   .   60

Loud conversation at 3 feet   Busy traffic .   70

Loud radio   Heavy traffic   Noisy factory .   80

Underground train   Motorcycle at 15 feet .   90

Very loud motor car horn at 15 feet .   .   100

Jet aircraft taking off   Work on sheet iron .   110

Riveting or pneumatic drilling, very close .   120   Pain threshold

Aircraft propeller at close quarters .   .   130   Painful sound

Identical measuring methods can also be applied for the sounds and noises of musical life.

On the whole, the dynamic range of music lies within the range of 60 to 80 decibel.

It must, however, be borne in mind that music is performed in large theatres or concert halls whose background noise is considerably higher than that of twenty decibel, given for the 'very quiet house' in the above table. Large numbers of human beings, if only by their breathing and the clothes-rub of their almost involuntary movements, increase this level very considerably. A German professor who has studied sound-intensity problems, and their adaptation for the construction of opera houses, stated* that he never has been able to reduce the background noise of his class of well-disciplined students to less than forty decibel.

In this context, the public of London's opera houses come in for praise: their chatty, pre-performance background noise of sixty-five decibel settles after a burst of applause greeting the conductor of about eighty decibel, to the commendable figure of approximately fifty decibel. An overture beginning in pianissimo at fifty-five decibel or so, can therefore be plainly heard and enjoyed.

This is not everywhere the case. The background noise of the famous Teatro del Liceo in Barcelona for instance, which during the chatty pre-performance phase is very much like that of Covent Garden, *fails* to settle to the London figure after the burst of applause for the conductor, and reverts to sixty-five decibel. This, of course, means that the background noise now cannibalizes the pianissimo entry of the orchestra, whose first chance of making itself heard only arrives when the music reaches a mezzoforte.

A list of measurements of sound intensities associated with music is given in the following table.†

---

* Personal communication from Professor F. Winckel.
† The measurements were taken (from front stalls mostly) with the British made ACOS SLM$_3$ and refer to the *A scale* decibel, db (A).

	Decibel
Very quiet concert hall or opera house	50
Solo instrument's (or voice's) pianissimo	55
Vocal *pp* acompanied by orchestra	60
Vocal *p* and orchestra	} 65
Softly played piano* in room	
People leaving after performance	65-70
Vocal *mf* and orchestra	70
Vocal *f* and orchestra	75
Vocal *ff* and orchestra	80-85
Piano played *ff* Strong applause	85
Big orchestral climax† e.g. *Frau ohne Schatten* crescendo	90
Piano *fff* in small room Clamorous applause	95
Vocal fortissimo at close quarters	100-110
Human voice's *ffff* very close to ear	120-125

Under free field conditions, where the sound waves spread in a sphere of increasing radius, all sound *intensity* is inversely proportional to the square of the distance from the source. As

* The measurements relate to a piano with open lid. Closing of the lid subtracts approximately 5 decibel.

† An Albeniz arrangement is said to have reached 100 decibel in New York.

sound pressure is inversely proportional to the distance from the source, doubling the distance from the sound source results in quartering its intensity and halving its pressure. This is equivalent to a six-decibel reduction in both parameters.

In an opera house with good acoustics this loss is mitigated by the sound reflections (see p. 84), and the loss of intensity between a front stall and a seat at the other end of the house should not greatly exceed ten decibel. Roofing structures over the heads of the audience (circles and galleries), can cause a disproportionate loss of sound intensity.

The singing voice, particularly that of the tenor or baritone, is in its fortissimo capable of an immediate loudness of up to 125 decibel, and many singers as well as repetiteurs have experienced discomfort and even pain in the ear when exposed to the full blast of a fortissimo at very close quarters. In the first act of *Tosca*, for instance, Angelotti, hugged by Cavaradossi, who sings *La vita mi costasse, vi salverò*, is exposed to a painful sensation of this type.

Voices of great strength are rare and occur at a rate of about one in 50,000.* According to the Registrar General's figures, approximately 800,000 births per year take place in England and Wales, which means that about 16 great voices are born every year. If the lifetime of a voice is 30 years, which is probably an over-estimate but a convenient measure as the 30-year span is the unit of the 'generation', 500 or so great voices of English and Welsh origin must be in existence at any one time.

In biological terms, and in accordance with its rarity, the great voice is an abnormality or rather a *variant* of infrequent occurrence. The mechanical reasons for the extraordinary power of a voice are not known; its power has certainly nothing to do with the shape or the strength of the vocal cords. It is due to

---

* While every care has been taken to base the figures contained in this section on reliable evidence, it cannot be claimed that they are statistically correct in a scientific sense.

particularly favourable conditions within the resonance area, which area imparts to the voice its beauty, its strength and its carrying power. This resonance area also determines the overtones which characterize the individual voices. The underlying anatomical and physiological circumstances which determine the character and the strength of the voice, are still very imperfectly understood. If one wishes to be scientifically honest, the only thing one can say is that beauty and strength of the voice are due to some lucky shape of one resonance area or another. It may well seem utterly deplorable that in our so very advanced days one has to remain as vague as that about so important a phenomenon, but it is nevertheless all one can truthfully say.

In singing a tune, the melody itself is a brain activity insofar as remembering it is concerned. The pitch which is produced is the result of consciously initiated, but subconsciously executed muscle action. Vocalizing is the limbering up of this muscular activity.*

Pitch fixation is governed by our brain, and can go wrong for two reasons. Firstly, because we can forget what pitch to sound (which can be compared to a failure to remember the words in reciting), or secondly, because gradation potential is not accurate enough. In the latter case we sing out of tune, either realizing that it is wrong, but unable to do any better, or, in other cases, not even realizing that it is wrong.

Singers with poor gradation potential are a conductor's nightmare. People with very poor pitch gradation, i.e. those who cannot perceive that the sound they make is wrong, had better leave public singing alone, though we certainly lose good voices through this irremediable defect. By listening attentively to the congregation's singing in church, we can

---

* This 'warming up' of the voice is considered essential by many singers. Failure to be able to do this within half an hour or so of singing, constitutes a hardship in certain operatic roles. Three of the four soloists in Beethoven's Ninth Symphony can warm up by singing the 'tutti' passages with almost closed mouth—provided no radio transmission takes place!

sometimes detect very fine voices of this unfortunate type.

Perfect pitch in singers is a much less frequent phenomenon than it is in conductors. It is, particularly if linked to a beautiful voice, a great asset indeed, and one English singer's impeccable intonation of difficult vocal lines has rightly made her famous throughout the world.*

The human voice possesses 'personal' quality to an amazing extent. We all know that it is comparatively easy to recognize over the telephone within a fraction of a second, the voice of someone whom we know only slightly, or someone whose voice we have not heard for many years.

It is more difficult to recognize a singing voice than a spoken voice. This is not only due to the fact that we generally know a person's singing voice less well than his speaking voice, but also because in singing part of the individuality of the speaking voice is lost, as the voice performs, i.e. it aims at a certain standard. In singing, some of those characteristics of intonation and inflection which, in speaking, add individual character to the voice are therefore omitted. Likewise, singing eliminates those highly individual mannerisms of speech which are so easy to recognize, the mannerisms which the clever imitator copies when he imitates the voices of well-known people.

In singing, regional and social accents too disappear to some extent, so that a person who speaks English with a Welsh, a Cockney or other accent will lose a good deal of this accent while singing. Foreign accents are more persistent because they are based on greater differences in vowel pronunciation than regional accents. However, even a foreign accent will be less obvious in singing than it is in speaking, a fact which facilitates 'phonetic singing' to some extent, though it does not solve all its problems (see p. 162).

---

* The respective incidence rates for perfect pitch are about one in four, or one in five for conductors—and one in several hundred for singers. The reason for this discrepancy lies in the fact that conductors are drawn to their career by their *musical* gifts, and singers by their *vocal* gifts.

The pronunciation of vowels is important because the vowels produce highly characteristic overtones, and the individuality of voices is based on the difference of their overtones. This partly explains the surprising fact that, considering the great differences which exist between voices, and the ease of recognition of an individual voice, the range of different voices varies much less than one might expect.

There are seven recognized differences of range, or *compasses* of the human singing voice, but as two pairs are practically identical, the actual number is reduced to five.

1.   The bass voice is the deepest human voice. Its typical range is:

Operatic work divides for reasons of sound-character, the bass roles into serious and buffo (comic) bass parts.

The value of voice sub-categories of all ranges is rather limited. These sub-divisions are all somewhat artificial, and as no voice equals another, the designations are variable and rather loosely defined. Over and above this, different countries use significantly different divisions, and a 'Heldenbariton' in Germany might well correspond to a 'basso cantante' in Italian usage.

2.   The baritone; his typical range is:

The main operatic varieties are the heroic (Helden), the lyric, the Italian (Verdi) and the comedy (buffo) baritone.

3. The tenor's range is:

but it is customary to note his music in the violin clef, and to read it automatically one octave lower (see p. 41).

The main varieties are the heroic tenor, the lyric tenor and the buffo tenor.

4. The contralto is the lower of the two female voices and also the lower one of the two boys' voices. The compass of both these voices is approximately:

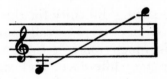

The explanation for the paradoxical fact that the lower of the female voices is called *alto*, i.e. high, is that the expression *contralto* stems from contratenor altus, the higher of that pair of voices whose partner was the contratenor bassus.*

The voice *above* the contratenor altus was the discantus, which later came to be referred to as the 'sovereign' voice, the *sovrano*, or

---

* A very old designation, appearing in manuscripts as early as 1450.

5. Soprano, which is the highest boy's voice (*treble*) and the highest woman's voice. The castrato (or *sopranista*) voice, too, had the same range, i.e.

The coloratura-soprano—a word of very doubtful propriety —(see also p. 188) should reach another third above, and sing F in the role of the Queen of the Night. Mozart is said to have used the ranges of his original performers when he wrote their parts. This caused him to extend Blonde's range in the *Entführung aus dem Serail* to:

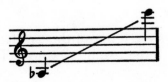

which presents a persisting difficulty for this part.

The 'mezzo soprano' is not really an acoustically well-defined unity. It is much more a timbre (overtone) quality difference than a range difference, and signifies that in this soprano voice the most beautiful part of the voice lies in its middle layer. The mezzo soprano can, in some respects, be compared to the bass-baritone of the male vocal range.

The sub-categories which are frequently overlapping, and are of particularly little value in the soprano range, are the dramatic soprano, the juvenile-dramatic, the juvenile lyric-dramatic soprano or soprano spinto, the lyric soprano, the lyric-soubrette soprano and the coloratura-soubrette.

The correct translation of the word soubrette is 'abigail', i.e. lady's maid. Baroque opera upheld quite strict social divisions, and the prima donna was almost invariably the lady of higher social rank. The soubrette was frequently her servant, a fixed relationship which is a relic, as well as proof of the soubrette originating in the *commedia dell'arte*. The *commedia dell'arte* was a very important improvised form of comedy in the 16th century: the *characters* in it did not vary, only the *situations* changed. Demand for this type of entertainment has always been great. probably for the psychological reason that it is easy for the audience to identify itself with the characters. Recently, this demand has increased to a remarkable extent; this is proved by the immense radio and television success of the 'series' type of programme (The Archers, etc.). These programmes are all a rather crude form of *commedia dell'arte* though it must be borne in mind that *commedia dell'arte* itself certainly was not highbrow either.

Analysis of the vocal ranges leads to the following conclusions:

1. The range of the human voice is approximately two octaves, though many exceptions exist to this rule: lately, compasses of as much as four octaves have come to the fore and surprised the public.

2. The higher a voice lies, the bigger its compass tends to be.

3. The difference between the bass and the baritone corresponds to the musical interval of the fourth.

4. The tenor's voice lies at least a fourth higher than the voice of the baritone.

5. In their typical ranges, the difference between the contralto's range and the soprano's range, too, is a fourth, and this difference equals the difference between the bass's and the baritone's ranges.

6. The difference between the contralto's range and the soprano's range, therefore, corresponds to the difference between bass and baritone, and *not* to the difference between bass and tenor which, particularly in its downward extension, is nearly an octave.

7.   The tenor voice holds a position of its own, and seems to be a phenomenon outside that male-female vocal symmetry, in which the bass voice corresponds to the contralto, and the baritone to the soprano. This asymmetry becomes obvious when one looks at the typical 'range pattern' found in most textbooks of singing, in which the tenor's range inserts itself like a wedge into an otherwise symmetrical pattern.

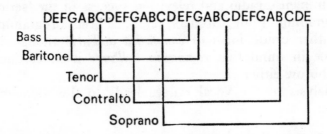

If these conclusions are correct, the tenor voice is a male phenomenon *without* a female equivalent, whereas baritone and bass are male voices *with* female equivalents.

The most convincing explanation of this position is that man is not born with a baritone's or a bass's voice: he begins either as a boy contralto or as a boy soprano.* During the period of puberty the larynx begins to expand and the length of the vocal cords increases. These changes occur so rapidly that the two vocal cords often expand unequally and cause the voice to crack. As soon as the new conditions are firmly established, the cracking ceases.

---

* For a long time it was held that a boy's voice made the most enchanting sound the singing voice could produce. Together with certain restrictions regarding women in the Catholic Church, this led to the hideous malpractice of castration. It constituted an excellent example of man's inhumanity to man which was only terminated as recently as 1911, when Pope Leo XIII decreed that there must be no more castrati in the Chapel of Papal Music (*Encyclopedia Universal* Barcelona, XII, 1912).

The descent of the voice is fairly fast, and the drop a very significant one. As the lowest sounds of the contralto voice are one octave higher than the lowest sounds of the baritone, the drop must be at least one of a full octave. If a boy soprano ends up as a bass, his voice has dropped *two* octaves. This drop, along with other signs of developing sexual maturity, occur under the influence of glandular activity.

The male-female vocal symmetry referred to above suggests that the tenor's voice is not a fully developed voice, but is the result of a prematurely arrested vocal descent, a descent in which the voice has not reached its normal, physiological terminus. This premature arrest occurs possibly as the result of malfunction of the endocrine mechanism which governs laryngeal expansion and enlargement.

If this theory is accepted, it becomes obvious why the male-female voice pattern is asymmetrical if the tenor voice is included in it, and why the symmetry is restored if it is excluded.

MALE	FEMALE
Bass	Contralto
(Bass Baritone)	(Mezzo Soprano)
Baritone	Soprano
Tenor	

If these deductions are correct, the tenor voice must be regarded as a 'variant', if not as a marginal abnormality. In a frequently quoted passage, the Italian writer Lucio d'Ambra in 1909 referred to the Italian tenor as 'the vainest creature in the world'.* It could well be asked whether the tenor's abnormality is associated with any other signs of dysfunction? Tenors are often accused of possessing difficult character traits and

---

* "... il tenore italiano è la creatura più vanitosa del mondo".

other peculiarities, but great tenors are glamorous, and glamorous singers incur the envy of the world, and readily attract all sorts of half-true and false rumours. In order to produce convincing evidence of linked behaviour characteristics, studies would have to be made on such large numbers of cases, and would have to probe into so much detail, that such investigations do not appear to be a practical possibility.

The above theory also clarifies the position of the counter-tenor. A countertenor can, with full voice, produce sounds which the tenor can only produce in falsetto register. It is, therefore, more or less a male contralto voice.* This phenomenon can be fully explained as a voice in which the arrest of the descent has taken place at an even earlier stage than it has in the case of the tenor. A fitting explanation for the occurrence of the 'male soprano', too, is provided: it is a voice in which the descent has failed altogether. The true male soprano is rare, and only very rarely is it of artistic value. It is utilized mostly for female impersonation and other variety acts.

It is not sufficient to be born with a good singing voice. One must also be aware of it, or must have been *made* aware of it. There is no doubt that many exceptionally fine voices have been left unused because their owners never thought seriously of singing, or, not being 'musical', were not attracted to singing. The musicality necessary to be able to sing in tune and to be able to memorize musical details is actually not at all rare: adequate gifts in this respect occur probably once in every 5-10 people, or at least 5,000 times more often than the great singing voices.

Some young people become themselves aware of their voice potential; others have to be told about it. Practically all operatic singers have loved and enjoyed singing from an early age. The

---

* The long vocal cords of the bass—broadly speaking, the lower the voice lies, the longer are the cords—can sometimes be made to vibrate in two sections, only one of them taking part in phonation: this can enable a bass to sing countertenor as well.

descriptions which successful singers give of the reasons which have prompted them to take up singing as a career do vary. Here are a few examples.

"I always loved to sing. Even when I was a schoolgirl I knew already that I could 'make a noise'."

The awareness of this being able to 'make a noise' sometimes has to come through others.

"I did enjoy singing, but what really made me think of taking it up properly was that my boyfriend at home said he could hear in the hills my voice far clearer across the valley than anyone else's."

"I always liked acting and impersonating others, and I also liked to listen to other people's singing. I once heard a tenor sing; I thought it was splendid, and I tried to imitate what he did. I did not really know how to. Someone said I should try and do it 'on the yawn'. I tried, and suddenly I knew it was there."

"I always sang when I was working at the factory, and someone whom I did not even know said: 'Did you ever think of taking up singing?' As a matter of fact, I had *not* thought of it, but I thought it was perhaps quite a good idea and I went to a teacher who later arranged for an audition."

"I went to a boarding school, and when I was about 15, my school joined up with a nearby boys' school to perform Mozart's Requiem Mass in C minor. I was offered the soprano part, and we rehearsed with the organist of the boys' school. Afterwards, he wrote to my parents and said that my voice should be trained."

Quite frequently the recognition of musicality and of love for music precedes the discovery of the voice. Some very good voices, particularly women's, were discovered when their owners were studying piano or another instrument at academic level, and unaware of their own potential in this respect, had opted for singing as their second subject.*

Which nation produces the best voices? Contrary to the prevailing and rather emotional views, the evidence available

---

* Kathleen Ferrier (1912-53) was made aware of her voice in this way.

on the subject strongly suggests that *the incidence of fine voices is fairly constant for all areas which the human race inhabits.* It has, however, already been stressed that a voice not only has to be there, it must also be known to be there, i.e. it must be discovered, either by its owner or by someone else. This leads to the crux of the matter. It is the *'discovery rate' which is the most important factor* in the recognition of potential voices, and this *differs significantly in different countries;* vast areas of the globe still have a very low discovery rate.

The importance of the discovery rate cannot be overstated, as some of the more recent events connected with singing prove very clearly. There is, for instance, no real evidence whatsoever that the actual incidence of good voices in this country has increased. The fact that many more operatic singers with very good voices are now coming forward is due to a much improved discovery rate. This, in turn, is the result of this country's generally much increased, as well as socially much extended, musical awareness.

The phenomenon of the 'Australian voice explosion' provides a striking example for the importance of the discovery rate. Australia has, of course, always produced great voices. However, in recent decades an unprecedented number of splendid Australian voices has made its impact on a surprised world, and perhaps on an equally surprised homeland as well. This is not the result of Australia's sunshine, her dryness of climate, the Italian immigration into Australia or of other nonsensical theories which have been put forward to explain the Australian voice miracle, but is merely due to the fact that her discovery rate, together with musical awareness in the country, has risen fairly rapidly; the backlog of previously unnoticed gifts in this direction may well have helped to increase the number of gifted singers who came forward within so astonishingly short a period.

The theory of the discovery rate also provides a correct explanation for the large number of good singers Italy has steadily produced over so many, many years. Again, this is not due to the sunshine or the olive oil, but merely to the fact that musical awareness in Italy has, since a very long time ago, always remained on a very high level: whatever the social background or the previous musical training of its owner, a really good voice was in Italy much less likely to remain unrecognized than in any other country of the world. The same applies to the Welsh nation. The Welsh do not breed more good singers than any other people, but their ubiquitous singing has kept the discovery rate very high, and it is rather unlikely for a promising voice to be overlooked. Conversely, it seems highly probable that the present scarcity of good French voices is linked to the fact that musical awareness in France—so different from the conditions at the turn of the century—is now passing through a period of relative indifference.

It is worth stressing at this point that the gift of the great voice is not necessarily connected with any other genetic or environmental musical traits. It is, for instance, independent of that most interesting musical gift, the inherited capacity to sing in harmony. This gift is in evidence in many mountainous districts, possibly because such areas combine love of choral singing with a certain amount of 'line' breeding. In Wales, in some of the Alpine valleys of Austria and Switzerland as well as in the province of Georgia of the U.S.S.R. a significantly greater percentage of the population than in other areas of the world are known to be able to sing, or rather improvise, in harmony. *Natural 'in harmony' singing is always improvised* and each execution of a song differs at least in some of its details. It is a remarkable phenomenon,* but certainly not linked to the occurrence of good voices in the operatic sense.

Once a country's discovery rate is high, good voices *are* found among all social strata. As singing is a 'gift' and the subsequent study pattern is extremely variable, singers show

---

* Scientifically, very little is known about this phenomenon, though it seems certainly interesting enough to warrant proper research. It is a 'phenotype' one, (i.e. genetic plus environmental).

enormous differences in their educational, cultural and social backgrounds. As a group, they are in this respect distinctly different from the instrumentalists or conductors. In whatever part of the world conductors or instrumentalists may have acquired their training, they have all undergone a period of professional study which in the different countries is conducted on very similar lines. Members of these professions, therefore, share many training and background characteristics, and are prone to conform in all countries to a certain pattern, as a result of the similarity of their education and social background. Conductors, in particular, often possess a very similar social, as well as a practically identical extra-musical and musical educational background. Their general knowledge, extent of education and even their social behaviour characteristics do not, as a rule, differ greatly between different nationalities.

All this is totally different in the case of singers. Their cultural background is subject to the greatest variations imaginable. Of two tenors who were alternately singing the same role in a production, one had been a professor at the musical faculty of a university prior to his operatic career, whereas the other had been selling petrol after a very sketchy general education. He held his job at a petrol station until a few weeks before his first, highly successful appearance in a famous opera house. Mario Lanza, an ex-lorry driver, quickly became the world's most famous tenor of his period, and many musical reference books report that Caruso used to earn his living as a flour bag porter.

As a result of this great variety of background and education, singers do not as readily correspond to a standard pattern as people in other professions do. Singers are of all sorts. Among them are people whose background is one of great wealth, and others who during their formative years had never enough to eat. Among them are extraordinarily erudite people, as well as some who can read only haltingly. One well-known soprano scraped with difficulty two passes at 'O' level together, while another, equally well-known, holds a university degree in theoretical physics.

Physically, too, there are enormous differences between them. As the result of a congenital deformity, one singer was never able to walk more than a few steps without severe pain, and the mere physical act of walking on the stage during rehearsals and performances caused an almost intolerable strain. Another well-known opera singer has represented her country successfully at many international sporting events, including the Olympic Games.

All these differences are augmented by the fact that various nationalities are likely to be represented whenever a few singers get together. These obstacles certainly do not, on the face of it, encourage that fully egalitarian and truly democratic atmosphere which nevertheless develops almost at once, wherever and whenever singers meet. Singers feel that they are linked together by a very powerful bond: they understand one another's unique physical problem of having to live with one's own voice. The voice which is an aspiration and an ideal, and often the envy of others, is at the same time a demanding tyrant and a tool of devilish extortion. More than anyone else, singers are utterly dependent on an unpredictable physical item of their organism, towards which they feel a terrible and compelling obligation.

The fear of losing his voice is never far from the singer's consciousness. Willingly he endures hardships for his voice, and the determination to serve it, to let it flourish, and to let it take its right shape and function, becomes almost an obsessive trait. This attitude to their voices is so important and so specific a feature that it draws singers closely together: they feel that they are all in the same, rather insecure boat.

For the non-singer it is very difficult to understand this position correctly. It may help him to think of the singer as a ventriloquist who is dominated by his puppet—the voice—as if it were an almost independent physical unit, a sort of small Siamese twin. This voice is a monster, insatiable in its demands and a cruel taskmaster to boot. There is no sacrifice that an ambitious singer will not be prepared to make on its behalf.

For many generations, conductors, repetiteurs and opera

directors have made the feudal 'jus primae noctis' suit their own
principle of 'jus noctis *first*', and have extorted their pound of
sex from young singers who took their fancy, with sufficient
consistency and bravura to knock every ball of the whole per-
missive society for six. Anywhere else such behaviour would
cause endless scandal, but in the singing profession hardly anyone complains: with a sigh of resignation, singers are often
prepared to be carnally exploited, provided that they are satisfied
that it is in the interest of their voice. No pleasure, no food,
drink or entertainment exists which they would not willingly
forgo for their voice's sake; no friend, lover or even husband or
wife, whom they would not sacrifice if the sacrifice is persistently
demanded by that monster within them. Neither artistic success
nor financial independence can break this bond of slavery.
Only *one* link proves strong enough to disrupt the slavery to
the voice, and this is the attachment of the mother to the born
(not the as yet unborn) child.

   In this servitude they feel terribly isolated. They can expect
no help and no real understanding from their conductor, nor
from their coach, and not even from their singing teacher unless
he or she has actually been a singer. With the best will in the
world, their spouses or lovers can only penetrate to the very
gate of this heaven or hell: the only people who really understand
them are their colleagues. This explains why singers, even when
they dislike one another, seldom or never become true enemies.
The chains of their fellow slavery keep them together.

   This explains also that exemplary comradery of a profession
where the famous meet the unknown with a cordiality quite
unrivalled among other professions. Jealousies and intrigues
occur in all professions; all the more frequently so in those
where one has to be personally selected for practically every
item of work, and where this selection depends on the whims
and fancies of a very small number of people. In spite of unavoidable jealousies and recurring intrigues, not only the outside
appearances are generally those of unequalled friendliness, but
true cordiality persists. Operatic singers are, in Mimi's words,

'senza rancore'. They know only too well what they all have to suffer.

Are operatic voices changing? A famous singer recently stated that because in the past the opera houses were smaller, and the orchestras much smaller (30-40 players instead of now 60-80), it is now far more difficult to sing 'above the orchestra'.

For centuries past, opera singing has been the true ambition of professional singers. To fill a large opera house with beautiful sound is not an easy thing to do, and a voice of sufficient power and beauty is given only to a few. There are other forms of music in which someone with musical gifts and understanding and with a beautiful, but not very large voice can make his mark. Such careers can give satisfaction as well as success and recognition, but operatic singing has always required a big voice. It is not true that the public's demands have increased and that in the past smaller voices sufficed.

As far as the size of the house is concerned, there are now many more big opera houses in existence than there were a hundred years ago. The great opera houses of Milan, London, Vienna and Paris have, however, not increased in size, and have sometimes even undergone structural alterations which improved their acoustic conditions. To be heard perfectly in every part of a big opera house requires no greater volume of sound now than it did before. What has changed is the demand for opera, and many more singers with big voices are needed now than were previously necessary. The actual singing requirements have remained the same.

As far as the size of the orchestra is concerned, big orchestras are now certainly in vogue, but the intensity of sound which the orchestra produces is not in direct proportion to its numbers. It depends on how the musicians are playing, i.e. on the way the orchestra is handled by its conductor. Only if an orchestra were to play at level intensity throughout would a direct relationship between the sound-volume and the number of players arise. A large orchestra, handled with skill, will never 'drown' a singer of sufficient voice, whereas even a small orchestra can blot out any number of voices if the brass instruments are allowed to overplay. Drowning of the voices is generally due to the conductor forgetting one of the golden rules of accompanying. This rule is that a voice can *for certain* only be heard by the audience if it can also be heard in the pit. If it cannot be heard in the pit, it may still be audible to the public, but not any longer with certainty. In the excitement of big orchestral climaxes during which the handling of the orchestra keeps the conductor fully extended, neglect of this rule can easily occur.

On the ladder of an operatic career, a big and beautiful voice is only the very basis for everything else. The singer must also know how to sing.

Is it possible to 'learn' singing? Before it can be attempted to answer this question, the argument has to be defined.

At the beginning of their careers, piano or violin players are faced with enormous technical problems. Only through qualified instruction over a long period and through concentrated study and application over an even longer period can these be overcome. When we compare the act of singing to the act of playing an instrument, the fundamental difference is at once apparent: the 'gift', i.e. the natural aptitude (the genetic aspect) is much more important in singing than in playing an instrument. It has repeatedly happened that a totally untutored, or hardly tutored singer has stepped straight from his natural singing into success on the stage of an opera house. Even if this is rare, it is an occurrence which could never take place in the case of the violin or the piano.

The purely technical aspects of singing are comparatively easily taught and easily learned. It is sometimes stressed that the basic technical requirements of singing contain nothing which a competent instructor could not teach, and a gifted pupil could not learn, during an afternoon's instruction. That may not be literally true, but in some cases at least it is not seriously wrong: the most important aspect of singing cannot be taught, it must be there. A variation of this is the truism that 'in singing there are no good teachers about—but some very good pupils'. This is not intended to be a criticism of the singing teacher, nor is it meant to imply that they are unnecessary. It is not easy to clarify this very complicated, partially obscure and rather emotive situation but some points seem worth noting.

Several big towns have been able to establish subsidized operatic training centres, where young singers are admitted whose qualifications regarding voice potential and musicality are not in doubt. One would expect that the young people trained there would be taught *singing*. This is not the case. They are taught almost everything else of musical or histrionic value, but they must make their own arrangements for their singing lessons and if they need them they must have them privately and elsewhere.

At first this may well seem a paradoxical arrangement, but it is really a sensible one. Every subject which the college teaches should be teachable, and singing does not quite fall into this category. If the combination of singing teacher and pupil is to do any good, it has to be a close relationship in which the element of choice and the need for a trial period are highly important. A singer can hear his or her own voice only incompletely, and, as it were, in a somewhat distorted way. He needs critical assessment of the sound which he makes, together with constructive suggestions regarding the possibilities and the mechanics of potential alterations and improvements. In some cases practically no changes or improvements may be necessary, and the voice is by nature perfectly projected. When this is the case, a singer can proceed to fame and fortune without much formal instruction. The majority of singer-students, though, need control and suggestions for changes. However, even experienced teachers are able to help with their suggested rectifying processes only in certain cases and not in others. This explains why the same teacher may be referred to as 'brilliant' by one pupil and as 'hopeless' by another, an assessment which by other pupils may well be given in reverse order.

The search for the teacher is a very personal one. The beginner craves to have his voice 'unlocked' and improved by the teacher's suggestions. Provided the basic gifts exist, this is sometimes possible, but no teacher can produce a singing voice which is not there. To assess and to accept his own limitations can be very difficult for an enthusiastic pupil. The case of the would-be singer without adequate vocal resources who goes from teacher to teacher is a sad, but not a rare one. The absence of a voice with operatic or concert potential should not, of course, discourage people from pursuing singing as a pastime: provided they accept the fact that they do not possess a 'marketable' voice, they will be able to please with their singing not only themselves but also their audience. Singing is, moreover, a splendid chest exercise and a healthy physical activity which can and should be recommended to everybody, and not be left exclusively to the professionals.

When singing is taught, it is generally done directly. Many textbooks on singing exist, but most books on singing are full of pathetic nonsense. Written by singing teachers, often those with charlatan's ideas, they try to impress the pupil with pictures of the larynx which neither the pupil nor the author can understand. Garnished with bits of gramophone records, extravagantly blurbed as standard text-books to be, they generally slide unlamented into that knacker's yard of the booktrade, the remaindering list. They paint a gloomy picture of the dangers of having one's voice 'ruined' by rival methods or by incorrect teaching, a threat which cannot materialize. No one can *ruin* someone else's voice, and all stories containing this expression must be taken with more than a grain of salt.

The story of the ruined voice is often a pitiable attempt to put the blame elsewhere in cases in which the voice was not big enough, or was not attractive enough to be successful. It is only human to be anxious to find a scapegoat for the missing success, for the success which was hoped for but which never came. The 'bad' singing teacher, who has ruined the pupil's voice or made him lose it, belongs to this herd of innocent scapegoats, though it is quite possible that prolonged attempts by a teacher to force a pupil to apply corrective measures which do not suit his case can have a bad effect and lead to prolonged difficulties.

In other cases the 'ruin' story has a different explanation. The singing voice is, alas, only a passing phenomenon. It can, and does lose its beauty or its volume at any moment through natural, unpredictable and irremediable processes, without needing anyone to 'ruin' it. To put the blame for the loss on to some person or action, may well be a psychological help in bearing such misfortune.

Additional to the technical needs are the singer's artistic needs. Some singers possess considerable, or outstanding, musical gifts, others are surprisingly lacking in musicianship, and yet can put a fine voice to splendid and successful use. Both require highly qualified musical guidance.

In the process of learning to play a musical instrument, technical instruction and musical guidance go hand in hand. In measure with the pupil's technical progress, musical guidance gradually assumes increasing importance over its technical counterpart. Technical instruction and musical guidance are complementary: the competent mentor will almost automatically teach both in their right proportions and at the right time.

The singer, unlike the instrumentalist, requires these two aspects of instruction in strictly divided manner: his requirements in musical guidance are such that, with rare exceptions, they cannot be met by the expert on the technique of singing. Although singers, merely by using their own gifts and aided perhaps by listening to other people, can forgo formal singing instruction, no singer can forgo musical guidance. Only one type of person possesses the necessary musical knowledge and the musical artistry to be of real help in this field, and this is the man with the training of the conductor, though he may well hold the appointment and use the designation of repetiteur or coach.* The repetiteur must be able to play the piano at least

---

* The expression 'coach' for a private tutor dates from the days of horse-drawn road transport: one took a coach to get on fast.

adequately: an outside pianist would infringe that intimacy of instruction which is so integral a part of successful teaching. He must also have a thorough knowledge of music, of vocal possibilities and musical literature. In other words, he must be a true 'maestro', even if he does not hold a conductor's post or does not hold a conductor's post *yet*: the repetiteur's work is a stepping stone for the conductor-to-be, who gains valuable experience through it.

The relationship between singer and repetiteur is a very special one. It fills a permanent need, and has no equivalent in any other aspect of artistic activity. In the visual arts, the painter or sculptor goes through a period of training during which he depends on experienced help and correction. Afterwards, he has to go forwards alone towards his own fulfilment. A virtuoso artist, a violinist for instance, requires regular help from a pianist for some of his work, but the pianist performs a *service* in such cases, and does more or less as he is told. The concert or Lieder singer's dependence on the pianist is of a more demanding type, nearer to a true partnership, and this has attracted outstanding artists to the art of accompanying.

The operatic singer needs the repetiteur in three ways: he needs him as an accompanist, he needs him as a substitute for the orchestra as well as for other voices, and, finally, for maestral guidance. The initiative is almost entirely on the repetiteur's side; the singer needs a person to whom he can hand himself over with confidence, and whose authority he accepts.

Opera houses have repetiteurs on their staff, whose duty it is to convey to the singers what the conductor of the performance will expect of them. He prepares them accordingly, but it is merely a facultative association. Most singers need a permanent link of similar type.

The relationship which can arise out of this need is a delicate one, because it is prone to mutual admiration and dependence. It has often led to intimacy and to marriage, and the shared interest can indeed serve as a firm link between the two partners. This is particularly the case if the relative position between them is maintained: this relative position is, at the outset, usually one in which the (male) repetiteur is experienced and competent, and the (female) singer at the beginning of her career. This is, of course, not necessarily an immutable situation. A Stendhalian reversal of the position arises if a singer is successful while her repetiteur husband remains static. The complications which such a situation can produce constitute one of the difficulties confronting the private life of the singer.

Ever since the days of the troubadours and their attending minstrels, singers have been expected to travel and to sing in other lands. This presents problems which can make it difficult to choose the right course. If the husband is a musician, though not of her standard, and she makes his taking part in performances a condition of her own appearance, she becomes guilty of a type of artistic extortion which may be tolerated and accepted for a while, but will never be fully welcomed and may ultimately rebound unpleasantly. If she takes her husband with her, but makes him merely her secretary or agent, he may eventually feel humiliated: it must be admitted, though, that at least in *some* cases this arrangement seems to work perfectly. If he just trails behind her, she risks forcing him into a ridiculous role—the husbands who are taken in tow by their prima-donna wives are regarded as pests in the opera houses. If she leaves him behind, she may have difficulties with him while she is away. Moreover, it is disenchanting for a singer having to 'unwind' on her own, and in many parts of the world it is rather awkward for a woman to go out alone, even if it is only for a meal, and suitable male escorts are not always readily available. The husband who is left behind might comfort himself with a vocally less important but possibly younger and prettier singer, perhaps subconsciously avid to recreate the circumstances of his previous happiness. There is no need to expound the inherent perils of such situations any further. Not many female singers have been able successfully to solve those problems; the male singer is much better off in this respect.

Whether singing is a desirable career remains open to doubt. If success is missing, the disappointment is obvious. Studying operatic roles, in sweat and in tears, without seeing any chance of using in the theatre what one has learned at home, only leads to disillusionment and bitterness. To join the chorus of an opera house is thrilling for a young singer, but it becomes a frustrating drudgery if it does not lead to the aspired promotion to a principal. Some singers have risen from the ranks of the chorus: many many more have failed in spite of their conviction that if only they were given a suitable chance they would be able to prove how much better they could sing than those whom they are permitted to 'cover'.*

Successful specialization in another field of singing is rarely possible for the unsuccessful opera singer. It is, on the whole, the successful opera singer who carries off the crown of the recital success as well. However, even the successful opera singer soon becomes aware that no interpreting artist's reputation is ever safe. At the beginning of every performance recurs the need to prove oneself all over again. The audience may prove enthusiastic, but is in many opera houses equally prepared to be outrageously cruel in rejecting the singer, should the opportunity arise, and a real or imaginary flaw appear in his performance.

The need to face a critical and potentially hostile crowd at every performance creates tremendous nervous strain. This nervous tension casts a shadow over the whole day of the performance, and every possible worry and uncertainty plagues and torments the singer.

The voice alone is always a problem. Many people regard singers as either hysterically, or at least as hypochondriacally obsessed with minor voice afflictions. If we take the trouble to examine the situation critically, the singer's pre occupation

---

* The traditional expression 'understudy' is now going out of use, as many singers feel it to be an offensive term.

with his voice is only to be expected and becomes readily understandable.

We are used to judge the problems of other people towards their own minor physical troubles by our real or imagined reactions in similar circumstances. It seems to most of us unnecessary to be unduly worried by a little cold or by a cough. What we overlook is that our own attitude to such indispositions is based on the conviction that our personal standing and the ability to earn our living is in no way seriously threatened by such minor incapacities. Incapacities of this type are, however, never minor ones for the singer, who at once sees his work, his career and his livelihood endangered. The awareness of real or imagined peril to our earning power is invariably a source of acute anxiety and of grave disquiet. It can, therefore, be readily appreciated that a cold or a little cough means something quite different to the singer than to the company director. The singer has to cancel his performances with the financial loss this entails, and has also —if it occurs repeatedly—to face the loss of reputation and good-will which his failure to appear causes. The businessman, even if he is a little husky, can still negotiate his deals and has no reason to feel imperilled.

The actor's position is significantly different from the singer's position in this respect. As long as his words can still be reasonably plainly heard, loss of clarity of the voice is of surprisingly little importance to the actor, and he can continue with his work successfully under conditions which, for the singer, completely rule out any performing engagement.

Some of the physical disturbances of singing occur un-expectedly; others beset the life of the female singer at regular intervals. It is generally recognized that the voice is prone to sound flat during the menstrual period. The reason for this is the loss of strength or 'tonus' of the abdominal muscles which occurs at this time. This fact is so widely accepted as a professional hazard that some singers stipulate in their contracts that they must not be compelled to perform during the days of their monthly period. It can, however, be readily appreciated that only artists of great international reputation, and not the rank and file, are in a position to impose such conditions. The singer has therefore to resort to the pill, so as to make at least the timing of those days when performances are likely to be sub-standard more accurately predictable.

Many other problems remain. Singing in a big house is a nerve-racking exposure. Its tensions can—like every manifestation of excitement—involuntarily increase the rate of respiration. This is particularly unwelcome to the singer, as it may force him, or her, to breathe at shorter intervals than during the more relaxed rehearsing period, and thus interfere with the intended musical phrasing. Excitement can also affect the faculty for the instant production, or the accuracy of memorized lines. This renders the provision of the services of an attentive and helpful prompter, in whom the singer can place absolute confidence, of great importance to an opera house.

After every performance, the psychological repercussions of these tensions continue and play out their own part. The day of the performance is the day the locusts have eaten: anticipation of the performance produces nervous tensions which exclude the ordinary involvement in those day-to-day activities which make a 'normal' day. Food does not taste, appetite barely exists, concentration on anything except the performance is difficult, rest is hard to find.

The performance itself acts as the great release, and only when the performance is over does the normal day begin. A feeling of relief and well-being is accompanied by the desire for food, drink and company: the unwinding process has begun.

This sets a special problem for those singers whose husbands, wives or friends may have to get up early on the following day. Few people feel after a full day's work that they would like to start the day afresh at 11 p.m., or later still. For singers of either sex, though particularly the female, unwinding is a definite problem. The matrimonial and extra-matrimonial complications which unwinding entails—even at home—are obvious, and they are intensified by the incessant travelling which the performances of artists in international demand necessitate.

When the unwinding process has been successfully accomplished, the ghosts of the previous night are still not fully laid. Post-performance-depression is prone to occur the following day. This phase of dejection is based on the factual or the imagined difference between the actual performance and an imaginary performance which the artist believes, correctly or incorrectly, that he could have given. It is a form of *esprit d'escalier** in an artistic sense, heavy with the sad realization of missed or lost chances. The resulting feeling of depression takes some time to be overcome, and its sting can be intensified by the reviews of the performance in the newspapers: few singers achieve complete detachment from 'the crits' in the press, however honestly they may try to convince themselves and others.

Not many people realize how difficult it is, merely to get the opportunity to appear in an operatic theatre. In order to show what he can do, the opera singer must be given his chance. Opera houses are most complicated and expensive 'machines' to run, and are, and perhaps rightly so, notoriously careful with their experiments. To begin with, the hurdle of the auditions has to be overcome. A suitable role has to be offered, under suitable circumstances. All these activities depend on persons and personalities which the singer cannot influence, or can attempt to influence only at her peril. Many sopranos have gone through permutations of Tosca's second act before they have ever had a chance to sing this role, and as the result of almost unavoidable personal experiences, the identification with the role of Tosca is said to be generally very easy.

And yet and yet, in spite of all these valid points against this career, valid points which should be most emphatically impressed on any person anxious to embark on it, few moments

---

* *Esprit d'escalier* means the realization—on going down the steps of a staircase, i.e. *too late*—of what one should or could have said to better effect during the antecedent discussion.

in life can possibly rival the superb feeling which follows the successful interpretation of one of the glamorous roles which the operatic stages has to offer. Singers amply deserve sympathy in their difficulties: they have to endure circumstances which would be tolerated in few other professions. We can, however, only envy them if and when that glorious moment of triumph arrives. To hear a roaring mass of public shouting 'bravo' at the top of their voices, and applauding as hard as they can, is, even if they are a foolish, fickle and ignorant lot, one of the most thrilling experiences the world has to offer. Yesterday's doubts, fears and troubles are forgotten. The next performance is still a few days away. The crowd cheers, and it is splendid to be alive.

Alas, it only lasts so short a moment.

SIXTH CHAPTER

VOCAL
TECHNIQUE

VOCAL TECHNIQUE

The similarity between the human larynx and certain musical instruments is frequently referred to, and is indeed obvious. The necessary respiratory effort, too, is similar, and the breath effort of singing is only a little less than that of playing a mouth-pieced instrument, e.g. bassoon or clarinet.

The only laryngeal effort of the clarinet and bassoon player is a modified respiratory one. The singer's larynx has to perform a complex series of technical functions as well, and has to emulate the technical dexterity of the clarinetist's fingers. The respiratory action as an automatic function is meanwhile in abeyance, though the respiratory need is overriding, and bursts through any laryngeal activity if the demand becomes compelling.

This puts the singer at a disadvantage in comparison with the instrumentalist, even the wind-instrumentalist. As a result of its twin functions, the larynx cannot always maintain that strict musical rhythm which forms the basis of an orchestra's sounding together or 'symphony'; a noticeable rhythmic laxity is bound to occur whenever the human voice enters an orchestral setting, and every conductor is well aware of this.

For clearer understanding of this situation it is necessary to review the technical commitments of the singer's larynx. These are generally referred to as vocal technique, and form something of a no-man's-land between the science of laryngology and the practical advice of the singing teacher. The subject of vocal technique embraces a multitude of problems and a maze of contradictory assertions.

The sound which the larynx is called upon to produce should
be well controlled and beautiful. Its pitch as well as intensity
depend upon acoustic pressures which are produced by muscular
contractions. These respond to impulses which have to be under
the singer's perfect control. The more precisely they can be
adjusted and technically perfected, the closer they will approach
the canons of vocal beauty. These can be summarized as follows:

VOCAL BEAUTY DEPENDS ON

1. Precision of sound, i.e. accurate intonation
2. Purity of sound, i.e. *position* of voice
3. Vocal range
4. Openness and evenness of timbre throughout the reach
5. A vocal adaptability which permits technical and
   expressive qualities to emerge freely

The method* through which vocal beauty can be achieved
is the vocal technique.

VOCAL TECHNIQUE ENCOMPASSES

1. Breath control
2. *Commencement* (*attacco*, or *prise du son*)
3. Passages and registers (or their elimination)
4. Falsetto
5. Timbre and colour
6. The so-called impostation
7. Vocal exercises (legato, agility, tone spinning etc.)

------

* Bettina Volpe's serviceable classification in 'Voce', *La Musica, Enciclopedia
storica*, V IV, p. 791, UTET, 1966, has been used in this chapter.

1. *Breath Control*

Respiration itself is an essential part of the mechanics of sound production. Of its two phases, expiration is obviously the more important one; however, all expiration is preceded by inspiration, and practice as well as opinion of individual singers and teachers regarding inspiration varies considerably.

It is claimed that only very few people breathe correctly. Details of breathing are therefore frequently taught, and various types of inspiration have been recommended. Many singing teachers and text books claim that slow and deep nasal inspiration not only promotes expansion of thorax and lungs, but also places the diaphragm into a specially 'sound-prone', low position, but this is nonsense. Whether any preliminary extra-vocal breathing exercises make much sense is doubtful: a strong case can be made for non-interference, and to let people do what comes naturally in this respect.

2. *Commencement*

Artistic function proper begins with the onset of vocal sound. In Italian, this is referred to as *attacco*, a 19th century expression, probably introduced by Garcia.* It has a somewhat misleading, aggressive connotation; the German term *einsatz* is less war-like. In English one simply speaks of commencement; pride of place, perhaps, belongs to the French term *prise du son*. Whichever term is chosen, it covers conflicting views.

According to Delle Sedie,† vocal phonation should always be preceded by a light inspiration in order to avoid an appo-

---

* Manuel Garcia (1805-1906), the inventor of laryngoscopy, the brother of Maria Malibran, and the most famous singing teacher of all time, published in 1847 his *Traité complet du chant*.
† Enrico Delle Sedie (1822-1907), well-known as baritone and as author, published *Arte e Fisiologia del Canto* in 1876.

giatura-type of grace note or the 'slackness' of humming. A different view is held by Garcia, who claims that the *attacco* is best performed with the sound of the vowel *a*, produced by means of the 'glottic thrust'. This is a deliberate glottic shock, comparable to a little dry cough, intended to give the vocal cords a 'shove'. It is rather at variance with physiological adduction which, under laryngoscopy, always appears gradual and even. From the physiological point of view it seems better suited to the larynx to begin phonation with a little preliminary breath.

As a corrective measure in cases of defective vocal *attacco* the use of explosive consonants has been recommended which, at the same time, is meant to school the voice in dramatic incisiveness and dramatic accent. Non-explosive consonants, too, have been suggested for vocal attack *en souplesse*, but are perhaps unnecessary for singers whose spoken language (e.g. English and German) provides sufficient opportunities of this type.

Certain movements of the lips, the tongue, the lower jaw and the palate contribute to the 'sound-readiness' of the vocal organ which follows inspiration.

According to the old Italian school, smiling and a hollowed out position of the tongue, similar to yawning, extends and enlarges the buccal cavity and resonance area. The recommendation to sing 'on the yawn' still forms a piece of sound advice which is given by many singing teachers. The compulsory smile, though, is now regarded as a useless, undesirable grimace, which impedes rather than aids the freedom of movement necessary for artistic expression. The spoon-shaped tongue, too, is no longer recommended because it is believed that it favours, rather than prevents, a nasal—instead of palatal— sound passage.

Slight opening of the lips, partial exposure of the teeth and a gently bent tongue with the tip pointing towards the roots of the lower incisor teeth is thought to offer the best conditions for free movement of the mobile sound-producing parts, and to ensure free access to all resonance areas.

3. Passages and Registers

Passagio originally meant musical ornament or *fioritura*. Later the term assumed a different meaning, and it now refers to the technical need to link, in the ascending as well as the descending gamut, the sound of one so-called register with the neighbouring one: this link is necessary as they are otherwise likely to sound somewhat different from one another. The expression 'register', first used in 1826 by A. B. Marx,* comes from the technical terminology of organ playing.

Whether the register theory should be accepted at all is doubtful. The old schools mostly list three registers: chest, falsetto and head. Some authors divide them into two: upper and lower. Mancini† speaks of the chest, and the falsetto or head register.

As far as their reference to the origin of resonance is concerned, these terms are, to say the least, imprecise. The two sexes differ to some extent in this respect as the male, with a somewhat lower larynx, has a more persistent chest resonance; even so, the low sounds too should emerge from the region of the hard palate. However, as during the emission of deep sounds the larynx lies somewhat lower, a certain amount of chest vibration occurs in any case. Any deliberate effort to let low-pitched sounds resonate in the chest, leads to an undesirable sound, a vocal distortion which the French call *poitriné*.

Equally imprecise is the expression head register: the resonance for the high sounds too, is predominantly palatal and sinusoidal.

---

* Adolf Bernhard Marx (1790-1866), a highly esteemed theoretician of music, became in 1850 co-founder of the Berlin Conservatoire.
† Giambattista Mancini (1714-1800), a famous castrato singer and teacher of singing at the Court of the Empress Maria Theresa, published in 1774 his *Pensieri e riflessioni pratiche sopra il canto figurato*.

With the 'vibrations by solidarity' which occur in response
to the primary vibrations, the whole of the body participates to
some extent in voice production. The primary vibrations all
originate in what the Italians call the *maschera*, the mask, i.e.
in the mouth, and to some extent in the chest.

Beyond all scientific and didactic controversy, however,
remains the fact that an uncertainty of the voice, a weakness or
sluggishness, occurs almost regularly between the highest low
sound and the medium sounds, and again between the higher
medium and the first high sounds. It is quite possible though that
this may be the result of wrong practice or of muscular weakness.

Correctly speaking, every sound which is being produced
must possess its own register. This register responds only to its
own proper stimuli, which are set into motion by the physiological mechanics of the sound-producing organ. It is interesting
to note that these physiological mechanics are so specific that
they enable some singers, who do not possess absolute pitch
hearing, to recognize tones correctly; if they attempt silently to
match the tone they hear with their own voice, their 'muscle
feeling' enables them to identify the tone.

If we accept the individual register theory for every tone,
it becomes doubtful whether the so-called 'covering' or *coprire*
makes sense. By this term is meant, or was meant, a tongue
movement which should extend the palate upwards, almost into
a triangular shape, and which, according to Garcia, can conceal
the assumed or true weakness between the registers. The same
applies to the so-called *closing* of the voice between middle and
high sounds, an even more artificial constriction of the resonance
channel.

Laryngoscopy, X-ray examination and many other investigations have failed to solve the register puzzle. In *Lavignac's
Musical Encyclopaedia* the opinions of five experts differ significantly, and Reynaldo Hahn* is the author of the well-known

---

* Reynaldo Hahn (1875-1947) South American by birth, French by upbringing,
  was famous as composer, critic and chief conductor of the Paris Opera.

bon mot: "If you want to know how many registers we have, don't read any books on singing!"

The factors which really matter are the suppleness of the whole sound-producing apparatus and a proper breathing technique. Voice registers are countless, and voice passages cannot readily be correlated to anatomical and physiological details. What is certain is that their elimination by good voice production is desirable, and greatly improves the individual timbre.

4. *Falsetto*

The so-called falsetto, too, forms a controversial topic. We do not even know the origin of this curious expression. It is thought that the term either comes from fauces, 'the voice which rings out from the fauces' or from *falsus* (false).

In favour of the latter etymology is Caccini's* recommendation (of 1608): in order not to have to depend on others, a singer should accompany himself on the theorbo (a large guitar) and should choose a tonality which permits him to sing in his full, natural voice, and avoid a 'false' or 'counterfeit' voice.

The subject of the falsetto is further complicated by the occasional use of the term to indicate the middle reach of both male and female voices, as well as by other wayward terminologies.

The facility to sing in falsetto is spontaneous, and difficult to learn. Falsetto gives the voice a considerable extension of the range which is of artistic use, and imparts to the male voice the potential to sing an octave higher than the true voice permits. For this reason alone, it assimilates the male to the female voice. This femininity in the character of the falsetto is less evident in the so-called rich voices. The falsetto can be made to sound

---

* Giulio Romano Caccini (1550-1618), one of the founder fathers of opera within the Camerata Fiorentina dei Bardi (see p. 49), published *Le Nouve Musiche* in 1602.

more robust by practice, and this leads to the 'falsettone', the big falsetto, a feature of the Bellini interpreter Rubini,* and later also of Gigli. The public cannot distinguish this sound from that of a true tenor.

The child's 'white voice', which boys as well as girls can develop from the age of six or seven and keep until puberty, is different from the falsetto. Its sound is probably due to the fact that during the phase of development and enlargement of the resonance area, the enlargement of the vocal cords themselves lags behind. The white voice does not differ in boys and girls, and does not depend on partial closure of the cords. It gives boys an extension akin to the falsetto, i.e. an octave above the corresponding adult voice, whereas girls, whose range is generally bigger than that of boys, only benefit by a fifth above their corresponding grown-up voice. The white voice has a certain chest resonance which the falsetto, of course, does not possess. Its characteristic chaste sound is due to its dearth of overtones.

5. *Timbre and colour*

The timbre is the 'physiognomy' of the voice. It is not only a distinction and a privilege, but also the one great advantage which the human voice possesses over all musical instruments. Timbre resists definition; it exists in limitless variety and it is subjective and unrepeatable. It is comparable to the character of the speaking voice (see p. 93) which possesses infinite personal quality.

Good vocal technique, it is said, will turn individual timbre into an asset, whereas bad technique presents it as a further liability.

The colour of the voice has nothing to do with its timbre, and is the result of the voice's playing with vowels. According

---

* Giovanni Battista Rubini (1794-1854), was known as the 'King of Tenors'; several of Donizetti's and Bellini's most important tenor parts were written for him.

to mood and meaning, vowels lend themselves to a great variety of modifications. The Italian vowels with their clear A E I O U, contain neither nasality nor guttural elements, and are, it is claimed, particularly fitted to a 'kaleidoscopic' technical-sentimental response.

Vowels are the result of the modifications which the sound undergoes when it emerges from the sound channel and passes through a pre-set lip position. This position differs for each vowel. The mood of the singer gives the vowels their shading, and one speaks of the 'colour palette' of a voice's expressive power. Such shadings are not distortions, but rather reflections of musical pathos as expressed in sound.

Sounds must not become standardized. Delle Sedie suggested that within the ten notes of one's *tessitura* (see p. 131) ten pre-set phonic vowel positions should be practised, ranging from the various *a* sounds over the *e* (open and closed) to the French *en* and *o* and *u*. Against this it has, however, been argued that a pre-set position robs the voice of that pliability which is necessary for its expressive power.

6. *Impostation*

Impostation means the setting of the voice into place and it, too, is a frequently misused term. If it has any physiological basis at all, it is the adoption by the laryngeal muscles of the most suitable position for the production of basic sound. Garcia maintained that impostation stands to gain by the use of those vowel-sounds which suit the individual voice particularly well.

The term impostation is also used for the *projection* (*indirizzo*) of the voice, which means its localization within the resonance box, i.e. really the voice itself. French authors speak of the *pose de la voix*.

This placing of the voice not only has its own problems but is also subject to gradual changes of taste. For example, throughout the 18th century it was the custom to slide to an intended note from a lower note, though from not more than a third below. This slide, recommended by Caccini, became unacceptable in the 19th century and was followed by Garcia's glottic thrust based on the vowel A. At present, commencement with a consonant linked to a vowel is recommended, and the tie-up between phonation and articulation is often stressed.

Again, what really matters is to bring out each voice's full and authentic timbre.

7. *Vocal Exercises*

Vocal exercises train the voice's freedom of movement and enable the voice as a musical instrument to deal with all types of vocal music.

The two fundamental exercises—equally important for all other instruments—are the legato and the agility exercises.

Legato is the basic requisite for all musical phrasing, and is closely linked to air volume and to laryngeal mechanics. To start with, it should only be practised with vowels. Later, syllables and simple phrasing in close intervals can be added. Close intervals are essential as only in the interval of the second can the voice *proceed*, without having to jump (see p. 143).

Legato is, as far as words are concerned, a vowel sound; most consonants are voiceless. Legato exercises focus attention on the time-value of the vowel which is being sung, and require rapid and clear enunciation of the consonants. This produces a sort of 'releasing' of the consonants which divide one syllable from the next, so as to pass without empty spaces to the next note. The 'sitting' on consonants, particularly those of passage, not only disturbs the continuity of the sound and distorts the phrasing, but contorts the word itself. Tunes which have one syllable per note are particularly dangerous in this respect. The opposite of the legato is the staccato (detached).

The so-called *portamento* from note to note belongs to the legato, and means sliding with varying sound-intensity from one note to the (more or less distant) next one. It is subject to the rules of good taste, and must correspond to the feeling which is to be expressed. All legato, of course, must, as an artistic necessity, stay attuned to the needs of expression.

Agility is the art of singing, at a desired and rhythmically measured speed, many notes on a single syllable or on a single vowel. It is an ancient practice, an important part of *bel canto's* formidable technical requirements. Mancini regarded it as a gift of nature. Some teachers valued it as the most important exercise for the diaphragm,* and for breath control, while others thought it bad for the power of the voice. To the agility exercises belongs the trill, an ornament which is very difficult to execute, particularly the trill on a single repeated note which at present is hardly ever heard. General laryngeal and mandibular flexibility is also required for the *arpeggi*, and for the diatonic and chromatic, ascending as well as descending scales, and especially for the *volatine*, the rapid scales.

The *suono filato*—the spinning of a note—consists of a single sound on a chosen vowel, which begins in pianissimo, becomes gradually stronger, and slowly reverts to pianissimo. For high notes it is somewhat easier to begin spinning from a lower note, to 'crown' it with the high note, and then return to the initial sound. Spinning was held to be the technical and aesthetic key to *bel canto*, the king-pin of all vocal exercises: it is still the most important exercise which the experienced singer (though *not* the beginner) should practise throughout his 'tessitura'. Tessitura too is a very frequently misused term. The tessitura of the singer is that inner compass within the singer's over-all range, in which the individual voice moves with greatest comfort and ease: it is, therefore, a more restricted range than the singer's full range between the low and high extremes, his vocal gamut.

The proper execution of singing's essential accomplishments depend as much on original talent as on the capacity to acquire technique by extended and laborious practice and application.

The classical vocal exercises were incorporated in study

---

* A misapprehension, as the diaphragm stays relaxed during such exercises.

compositions which charmingly reflect the changes of musical taste. Every period had its own vocal ideal, and this vocal ideal has passed from Rossini in the early 19th century by way of Bellini and Donizetti to Verdian dramaticity, with all its vocal requirements. Not every period has, however, created its own introductory studies. The period of *bel canto* has produced many musically valuable studies, particularly the twelve Ariettas which Vaccai* published. Rather surprisingly, Verdi's and Puccini's periods have failed to produce corresponding pedagogic material.

The last decades have witnessed a great vocal revolution. The vast repertory of the present theatre expects from singers a musical versatility which their predecessors, who executed mostly contemporary works, did not need to possess.

Nothing has, however, altered the basis of *bel canto*'s vocal aesthetics. The singing voice must keep in time, but, unlike other musical instruments, it cannot be used to beat time. All metric accents are to be avoided, and, in order not to interfere with the respiratory function of the larynx, the voice should never be given any accent which is not in the text.

It is because they express intuitive respect for physiological facts and principles, that the fundamental rules of *bel canto* have remained, and will remain valid, as long as the enjoyment of singing lasts.

---

* Nicola Vaccai (1790-1848) composer and singing teacher. He taught in London in 1832. The proper title of the work above referred to is: 12 *Ariette da Camera per l'insegnamento del bel canto*.

COMPOSING
AND COMPOSER

COMPOSING AND COMPOSER

To compose means 'to put together'. Musical composing began as the putting together of a 'cantus firmus' with other voices, a work performed by master craftsmen who were capable of varying, suitably ornamenting and combining the musical lines in this process. The 'cantus firmus' (see p. 35), the 'fixed song', was either freely invented or taken from another piece of music. It formed the basis of the composition.

Composition of music was preceded by musical improvisation. The music of the ancient world used to be regarded entirely as improvisation, but it has recently been pointed out* that a passage in Plato's Laws suggests an activity which is very closely related to composition indeed. This passage complains of people "who mixed songs of sorrow with hymns, mixed paeans with dithyrambs, who imitated aulos music [i.e. wind-music] with stringed instruments, and who judged music by the pleasure which results from it".

Musical notation in the modern sense developed out of cheironomy (see p. 21), possibly by way of pictures of musicians engaged in giving the appropriate signs. Music served a ritual purpose, and early notations may well have been made in order to prevent liberties in improvisation from reducing the ceremonial effect of the ritual. These beginnings were in fact a *codification of the results of improvisation* rather than composition proper.

Improvisation continued to play an important role until the

---

* Georg Knepler, 'Improvisation—Komposition' *Studia Musicologia Acad Scient. Hung.* II 1969.

beginning of the 19th century. The 'classical' realization of the continuo bass, the musical ornaments of singers and instrument-alists, as well as the concert cadenzas are all suitable examples of improvisation. It is interesting to note that after a long period of neglect during which only the organists availed themselves of its potential, it has lately (since 1950) again become an important factor in musical composition.

The exceptional ability of Bach and Mozart for musical improvising has been amply recorded. The variations based on traditional chorales and on tunes of other composers still played a decisive role in Bach's compositions. Musical invention and musical fantasy became progressively linked to all musical formulation. In the course of the process during which the art of putting music together became the art of the *invention* of music (i.e. during the gradual conversion of music into an 'ars inveniendi' in a modern sense), two events proved of particular importance: the discovery of equal temperament, and the development of the 'orchestral language' with its consequential reduction of the continuo's importance.

The tempered keyboard instrument was a step forward of greatest significance. Instruments of fixed pitch have always been particularly useful to the composer, because they allow many more notes to be sounded at the same time than any other instrument. However, unrestricted modulation from one key to another was impossible until the beginning of the 18th century, because the resulting dissonances were disturbing. These dissonances are caused by the fact that the division of the octave into 12 chromatic steps is an artificial and arbitrary one. In order to produce sounds without noticeable dissonances, 53 gradations within one octave would be necessary, and, not surprisingly, the construction of such an instrument proved impracticable.*

The physical reason for the dissonances are the irregularities,

---

* It was attempted by Bosanquet in his "Keyboard Harmonium", and experiments in this direction are at times still being made.

or 'commas', which result from the mathematical structure of the tone scale. These commas have a reputation of being most difficult to understand and to explain, and a comparatively simple explanation is proffered herewith.

Our scales are built on the basis of definite frequency ratios between the notes which follow one another. Their sequence must be acceptable to the ear. In the diatonic major scale, where seven notes are distributed unequally over the octave, these tone intervals, established since ancient times, are as follows:

TONE INTERVAL	NOTE SYMBOL	FREQUENCY RATIO
First	C	1
Second	D	10:9
Major third	E	5:4
Fourth	F	4:3
Fifth	G	3:2
Major sixth	A	5:3
Major seventh	B	15:8
Octave	C	2

The most important tone intervals are grouped into consonant and dissonant intervals:

CONSONANT TONE INTERVAL	RATIO	DISSONANT TONE INTERVAL	RATIO
Twelfth . . .	3:1	Major seventh . .	15:8
Octave . . .	2:1	Minor seventh .	9:5
Major sixth . . .	5:3	Minor sixth . .	8:5
Fifth . . .	3:2	Major whole tone .	9:3
Fourth . . .	5:4	Major semitone .	16:15
Minor third . . .	6:5	Minor semitone .	25:24
Unison . . .	1:1		

The dividing line between consonance and dissonance is subject to a gradual change towards consonance. The minor sixth and the minor seventh, for example, were by the 19th century no longer felt to be dissonant.

It can be proved by two different methods that these intervals are not entirely accurate.

I. The compound interval of the major ninth, e.g. C-D

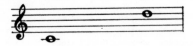

can be reached by two different steps: either by dividing it in two fifths, i.e. C-G and G-D

which would give 3/2 . 3/2 = 9/4, or, by dividing it into a major sixth and a perfect fourth, i.e. C-A and A-D

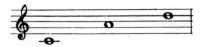

which gives 5/3 . 4/3 = 20/9.

This results in two different figures for the same D as 9/4 and 20/9 are not quite the same. The product, i.e. 4/9 . 20/9 = 80/81 leads to the difference which is 81-80/36 = 1/36. This is the comma of Didymus,* or syntonic comma.

---

* "Bronzebelly" Didymus (63 B.C.-A.D. 10), so nicknamed on account of his unprecedented capacity for work (also called "Bookforgetter" on account of his poor memory for his own output), lived in Alexandria, where he is said to have written 4,000 books, fragments of which survive. He upheld the musical theories of Pythagoras against Aristotle.

II.   The second method, too, reveals a significant discrepancy. Every octave, 2:1, must consist of six whole-tone steps, (seconds, 10:9), but $(10/9)^6$ is $1,000,000/531,441$ and not, as it should be, $1,000,000/500,000$, i.e. 2:1.

If from any given tonic we work 12 fifths upwards, i.e. if we proceed along the full 'circle' of fifths (see also p. 147), we return to the tonic seven octaves higher up. Again, the twelve fifths, as against seven octaves, give different results. This difference is referred to as the Comma of Pythagoras, or the diaschismatic comma. A minute difference exists between the two commas. This difference is called the schisma, and it corresponds to the difference between 32805 and 32768. (See also p. 140.)

The commas do not produce serious difficulties for the stringed instruments: the violinist who is playing consecutively C, A and D, varies almost automatically either the sixth or the fourth, otherwise the resulting 'D' would not tally with his D string. The difficulty which the commas presented for the fixed-tone instruments, particularly for the instruments played by claves or keys (Klaviere) is quite obvious. That these instruments could not modulate freely from one key to another has already been mentioned. Certain modulations provided particular difficulties.

The whole problem was solved by Andreas Werckmeister (1645-1706) who in 1691 successfully proved that the comma could be evenly divided between the intervals of the octave at the rate of one twelfth of the comma to every semitone step. This led to several important results.

1.   Strictly speaking, none of the intervals were any longer really 'correct', though they were not disturbingly incorrect either.

2.   C sharp now became the same as D flat, and enharmonic changes on all levels became possible, so that

3.   on a 'fixed tone' instrument it now became possible to make music in all keys, and

4. one could modulate freely from one key to another.

5. The interval of the third, previously considered to be a dissonance, now assumed consonance.

The fundamental element of measurement of musical intervals is of course the octave, with its proportion of 2 to 1. Equal temperament brought about the necessity to divide this interval into a number of equal fractional units. Euler* was the first, in 1739, to devise a logarithmically based unit of this type. Other units followed later, some attempting the division of the octave on a decimal basis, others on a duodecimal basis; the latter ones proved more serviceable because the octave can be divided in 12 equal semitones.

The modern unit is the cent, and each octave is divided into 1,200 cent. Each semitone of the tempered scale corresponds, therefore, to 100 cent, and each quarter tone to 50 cent.

The commas, too, can be expressed in cents. The comma of Pythagoras is approximately 24 cent, the comma of Didymus 22; the schisma being therefore 2 cent. The finest difference which the human ear can detect under absolutely ideal conditions in every respect is 6 cent.†

Werckmeister's invention proved most beneficial to the art of composing. The first work published for the newly 'moderated' or 'tempered' keyboard was *Ariadne Musica* by J. Fischer in 1715. Fischer's example was followed by Bach in 1722 and 1744 with the two volumes of his *Wohltemperierte Klavier*: this was a collection of 48 preludes and fugues in chromatic ascendance, beginning with C major and C minor, a work referred to by Bülow as the *Old Testament* of Klavier literature. (The *New Testament*, according to Bülow, are Beethoven's 32 piano sonatas.)

---

* Leonhard Euler (1701-1783) Swiss mathematician.
† This, however, does not take into account the phenomenon of heterodyning, in which the marginal difference between two *simultaneously audible* sounds becomes recognizable through the physical manifestation of 'beats'.'

It is in this connection relevant to point out that the German word 'Klavier' cannot be fully equated to the word piano. The clavichord (a piano ancestor) and the harpsichord (a very indirect piano forerunner) are both Klaviere, but they are *not* pianos. The *Wohltemperierte Klavier* was not written for the piano: parts of it were written for the harpsichord, a quill-plucked instrument to whose family the English virginals belong as well (see also p. 19). Other parts (especially the Preludes) were written for the clavichord, whose attractive but small sound precludes it from being used in a large concert hall: it can hardly be heard through closed doors.*

The piano is a Klavier with hammer action, an action which was already in use for the cymbal. Since the beginning of the 18th century, the hammers which struck the strings of such instruments were worked by means of keys. The immediate precursor of the piano was the 'Pantalon', and hammer-powered pianos in a large variety of types and names and in diverse shapes (Richard Wagner used a 'desk-piano' which was particularly suitable for the rapid change-over from playing to writing) and differing methods of sound-production quickly established themselves as instruments of predilection for the composer's studio.

The hammers were lined with leather or with felt, and after hitting the strings they fell back quickly. The striking of the chords *produced* the sound, and the felt cladding damped the sound. The sound which was produced by *striking* lasted considerably longer than the sound which, in the case of the harpsichord, had been produced by *plucking* the strings. Moreover, the new pedal could obliterate the damping action of the cladding and enabled the tone to ring out without restriction. The main innovation, however, was that the new hammer action permitted a gradation of sound intensity; the sound rose and fell

---

* Its sound is produced by the keys moving an iron 'tangent' on to the string, and making the string, or part of it, vibrate; this action establishes the clavichord as a true piano ancestor.

according to the force with which the hammer struck the strings. This development gave the new instrument the power of crescendo and decrescendo, akin to that of an orchestra, and also gave it a new name, the Gravicembalo (later also Clavicembalo) col piano e forte, which in due course was abbreviated to piano forte or fortepiano, and eventually simply became 'piano'.

At the beginning of the 19th century two different types of hammer action were in use. In the 'Vienna' action the hammer struck the string from below and the pianos thus constructed were of pleasingly light touch and gracious sound. Mozart used a piano of this type.

The 'English' action was different. The hammer was not pushed but flung against the string, which gave a far greater sound. The sound could expand even further when a cast iron frame permitted the strings to be placed under greatly increased tension. It should be regarded as a source of pride and satisfaction by the English that in 1818 Messrs. Broadwood, with a characteristically English mixture of business acumen and generosity, presented Beethoven with one of their newest instruments. It was his greatest delight.*

New possibilities presented themselves to the composer. The freedom of symphonic development, as well as the recession of the rather restricting figured bass which followed Haydn's new ideas of orchestral sound, contributed to the enormous progress which symphonic music made in the 19th century. Advances in the construction of orchestral instruments greatly increased their technical as well as their expressive potential, especially of the wood-wind instruments. New sound variations such as the mute for strings, the trumpets and the trombones,

---

* The present Chairman Capt. Evelyn Broadwood, MC., explains that such gifts were made by Broadwoods to important composers 'pour encourager les autres'. As Beethoven was not really able to pay for the transport, the piano was sent carriage paid. Upon Beethoven's death, the piano was bought by a secondhand dealer, from whom in turn Franz Liszt purchased it. Liszt left the piano in his will to the Museum of Budapest where it is now exhibited. According to Capt. Broadwood, it is in perfect working condition.

stimulated the art of orchestration. Scoring reached new heights with Berlioz who, while still a medical student, displayed quite unequalled genius in this comparatively new field. How advanced his ideas were can be appreciated if we compare his scoring with that of Verdi, who at the very same period still used the orchestra as a giant guitar.

The advent of the tempered scale had affected the stepping- and building-stones of music: the intervals. Even these began to change in significance.

The second is the only interval whereby the human voice can 'proceed' rather than jump. The rising second expresses overflowing sentiment. The second, therefore, has always been the preferred interval for singing, particularly for the bel canto, in which the sound aims at absolute beauty, as well as at fullness and smoothness of melodic progression.

On account of the comparative harshness of the German language, it was in Germany realized quite early on that word and sound are two independent and unequal elements, which can never be perfectly combined. This led to the striving for sound 'to fit the content of the word', which made singing gradually less dependent on the interval of the second.

In the Pythagorean tuning the third was regarded as dissonant. As a result of equal temperament, it now made the grade to consonance. The third is the decisive factor in the major-minor tonality. For this reason it became a particularly favoured interval for the music of the Romantic period and for the true 'popular' tunes or folk tunes, i.e. types of music in which the major-minor tonality was of special importance. The traditional reluctance to let a piece of music continue in minor tonality to its end, led to the use of the 'Picardy third', which is a major third terminating a piece in minor key. This custom is believed to have originated in Picardy.

In atonality the third is not a desirable interval at all, and therefore avoided.

London's fire engines warn the traffic in a descending major third, and ambulances race to accidents and hospitals while sounding a descending major third which seems at times to change into a minor third.

The fourth has for a long time been a conundrum of music. The question as to whether it was an interval of consonance or of dissonance presented a problem which was resolved only by our generally changing attitude to the dissonance. Wagner used the fourth for his characterization of Beckmesser. In the 20th century the 'neutrality' of the fourth (it is inconclusive as far as tonality is concerned) has made it desirable, and for Bartok as well as for Stravinsky it became a favourite interval.

In its emotional content, the fourth has always been a call to battle. British Railways' new diesel engines use a descending fourth as a warning signal. Many European fire brigades use an ascending fourth as their alarm signal.

The augmented fourth forms the tritone, the interval which divides the octave into two equal halves. This interval received the unflattering title of the *diabolus in musica* (the devil of music) as it is a very difficult interval for the singer to pitch correctly.

The fifth is an interval of special importance as the tonic of the dominant chord. The empty fifth sounds ghostly, and it is frequently used just for this effect, e.g. in the overture to *The Flying Dutchman*. Many 'devilish' pieces contain empty violin fifths (see p. 54). Most stringed instruments are tuned in fifths (in pure fifths in fact) although theoretically they should be respecting their share of the comma's temperament. The difference between a pure fifth (3-2) and a tempered fifth is also referred to as a schisma. It is almost identical (a shade smaller) than the schisma mentioned on p. 140: it is 1.6 cent.

Atonality deliberately avoids the emotional content implied in the intervals.

Some modern schools favour intervals beyond the octave, and as intervals beyond the ninth or eleventh are no longer heard as a 'sound relationship', their usage has led the way to Germany's 'Punktuelle Music', the pointed, i.e. 'disjointed' sound relationship.

The characteristics of the individual keys, too, were keenly scrutinized.

Already in the church modes of the 16th century some modes were regarded as cheerful and others as sorrowful. The equal temperament permitted the use of many more keys, and their indefinable associations form one of the most controversial aspects of music. All these 24 major and minor keys, which could now demonstrate their full individual characteristics, consist essentially of the same sounds. Different composers have expressed strikingly different views regarding these same keys. Johann Matheson, who in 1739 published his *Perfect Conductor*, the most important musical textbook of the period, thought that E major expressed utter despair. Berlioz regarded the same key as lustrous, splendid and noble. It is perhaps not surprising that Richard Wagner regarded all these characteristics as being quite 'chimerical', although later it was thought significant that *Lohengrin* was written in A major and *Parsifal* in A flat major.

It has been suggested that it was typical of Haydn's character that he generally used only the simple keys with at most two sharps or flats, most commonly C, G and D major. For Mozart, G minor certainly had a profound and sad emotional association. Beethoven stated explicitly that he had chosen the keys in *Fidelio* with great care, and that he thought the G sharp chord gave Pizarro his individual characteristic. Beethoven's works suggest that D major and D minor were his favourite keys. F major has often been regarded as 'nature's key'. The 'Pastoral' Symphony is written in this key, and it has been contended that all waterfalls roar in F major, at least in Germany.

During the Romantic period of music, from Chopin to Debussy, six or so flats or sharps were in frequent use. Hindemith made use of different keys to identify particular persons, feelings and objects.

A certain degree of key-change occurred more or less unintentionally with the recent changes of the concert pitch. Everything, of course, depends on the standard A. This has

varied considerably during different centuries. It seems likely
that the high concert pitch which is now generally in use makes
us hear the symphony which Beethoven intended to be a C
minor symphony, in C sharp minor. The fact that it nevertheless maintains C minor sound-characteristics has been used
to support the contention that key characteristics are valid and
real characteristics, after all.

The situation is further complicated by the fact that different
instruments are prone to sound more natural in some keys than
in others, and 'God Save the Queen', John Bull's* *National
Anthem*, can be used to exemplify this. By the very nature of
the occasions, its execution is generally the prerogative of brass
bands. For reasons connected with the brass's natural air columns
(see p. 41), B flat is a favourite key for such renderings, and
gives a very satisfactory sound.

However, if a symphony orchestra is playing the *National
Anthem* in B flat, it will sound a little vulgar. In accordance
with Monteverdi's law regarding the need for preponderance of
the strings (see p. 50), it will sound more elegant if the fundamental one of the stringed instruments is used to indicate the
key. Quite properly, therefore, symphonic orchestras play the
National Anthem generally in G.

The claim for the relative or successive characteristics of
keys is much better documented. The change from C major
to A major and on to F minor, for instance, expresses a definite
and characteristic sequence of tensions.

The 'fifth circle' of rising sharp keys conveys an increase
of tension (C—G—D—A—E—B—F sharp) and its equivalent

---

* The *National Anthem* was, most probably, composed by John Bull (1562-
1628), one of the foremost composers of his day, particularly of music for the
keyboard. It was published as an 'Ayre' in 1619, and remodelled in 1740 by
Henry Carey. Words and music first appeared in print together in the 'Gentle-
man's Magazine' of October, 1745. It proved a most popular 'official' tune
and was, fitted with appropriate verse, used at some time or other as national
anthem by Denmark, Germany, Switzerland and, until 1931, by the U.S.A.

flat range relaxes tension (G flat—D flat—A flat—E flat—B flat—F—C).

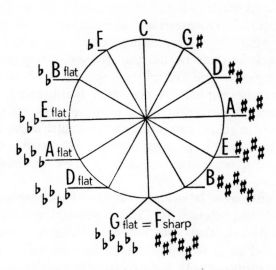

The characteristic effect of the change from a major into a minor key has been known for a long time. The change from C major to A minor and back makes a musically characteristic statement. Composers soon knew how to make use of the new possibilities which the tempered keyboard had given to music by permitting all modulations in major and minor keys from every tonic. Schubert used the change from major to minor to display that 'double meaning of life' which many of his songs so tenderly reveal, and he often closed a piece in a minor key with a Picardy third, with very touching effect indeed.

During the Romantic period, composition was regarded as something which had been given to the composer *in toto*. Foremost among those composers who possessed the gift of letting whole pieces of music grow within themselves, was Mozart: he could carry three complete and different works in his head before eventually writing them down in one 'go'— another aspect which reveals Mozart as the inexplicable miracle. Other composers who possessed this gift include Schubert and

Hugo Wolf. Returning from a walk, Arnold Schönberg once
wrote almost 100 bars of twelve-tone music straight down. The
incredibly rapid work of some of the great Italian operatic composers, particularly Donizetti and Rossini, can only be explained
by the fact that they, too, could carry a complete or almost
complete work in their heads, though not infrequently a fairly
considerable part of such rapidly completed work was repetitive
rather than truly original. On the other hand, many composers,
Beethoven and Brahms among them, never wrote a whole work
at one sitting. In many instances, the thematic ideas for a single
work of theirs not only presented themselves with long intervals
in between, but were also worked out most painstakingly and
gradually.

Composing as a laborious process of putting together has
remained of importance for most musical efforts, and the
plaintive witticism that creative composing consists of 10%
inspiration and 90% perspiration has in turn been attributed to
many great composers. In a conversation with Heinz Tiessen,*
Richard Strauss expressed his own views on this point with
touching modesty and great clarity: "The ideal is the great
melody, streaming out by itself, as it were. Mozart had it, and
so had Wagner. I'm afraid I have *not* got it. Mostly only four
bars come to me, or, at the best, six or eight. And then the
composing starts." This, according to Tiessen, is Strauss'
confession of his 'aspiration to the ideal of the great line which
has grown by itself without having had to be worked for'.

From the beginning of the 17th to the beginning of the
20th century tonality remained the body and soul of harmony.
The basis of tonality is the division of the octave into the
diatonic 7-note scale, which contains 12 semitone differences
in its chromatic sequence. The position of the third makes the

---

* Heinz Tiessen (born 1887), conductor, Director of the Berlin Conservatory,
  known for his interest in nature's music and his work *Sound language and form
  of the song of blackbirds*.
  Internationale Richard Strauss Gesellschaft 54/55, 1967, p. 26.

significant difference between the simple major system of tone
—tone — semitone — tone — tone — tone — semitone, and the
rather less homogeneous minor systems. A composer could
choose the key whose tonic produces the centre point: all chords
then stand in significant relationship to one another.

During the second half of the 19th century the strictness
and the strength of this system began to flag. The use of the key
signature alone has never been entirely reliable as an indication
of the key in which the music was really written: only the final
chord of a work permits the classification of its key. In some of
Beethoven's works* the basic key only gradually becomes
apparent. The First Symphony begins with a modulation which
pretends to move towards F but turns out to be an extended C
major cadenza. In the Prelude to Wagner's *Tristan*, which has
the key-signature of A minor, the A minor chord does not even
sound once. In some works of Chopin the question of the key is
left altogether undecided.

The restrictions which the rules of tonality imposed became
increasingly irksome to the composers. The beginnings of
atonality can be traced to the free harmonies of *Tristan*, and it
has even been contended that atonality itself was conceived in
that moment at the beginning of the second act of *Tristan* when
alternating horn signals back-stage intermingle C minor and F
minor in revolutionary fashion.

A further stage was reached through the startling sound
effect of the six-note chords which Debussy, who was the first
composer to experiment with the whole tone scale, as well as
other Impressionists obtained by laying two different keys on
top of one another. This made bitonality a new musical principle.
Hindemith and Stravinsky, while adhering to the tonic as a
tonal centre, founded a new in-between stage of musical writing,

---

* The slow movement of the Piano Sonata op. 10 carries the 6-flat signature of
  E flat minor, but is actually written in A flat minor.

in which, for example, a symphony was stated to be in E flat, instead of in E flat major.

The next step, polytonality (multiple tonal centres), led to atonality (no tonal centre) as its logical conclusion. Schönberg's and other composers' replacement of the third by the fourth in chord construction was perhaps the decisive step. In atonality, the twelve notes stand, without a centre, next to one another in absolutely equal rights. Schönberg moulded this free atonality into a new system, the Twelve Note System.

In the wake of this new system came the conception of the 'free articulation', a new word-rhythm which broke its links with musical meter in the ordinary sense. The ultimate fulfilment of atonal sound is the simultaneous sounding of all twelve notes, an effect which was achieved in the final chord of the German composer Klebe's *Lullaby*.

In succession to atonality, electronic music has now become the latest musical language. Free from all tonal associations, it can be divided into two categories: either the sound is created entirely by electronic processes (synthecized sounds), or natural sounds, in particular voice and percussion effects are manipulated by 'electronic distortion' (musique concrete).

The new trends and developments in no way reduced the need to study the fundamental rules under which music was composed between 1600 and 1900, the era which produced the core of our musical inheritance. The abrogation of many of the old rules of composing has not made his work easier for the modern composer. His knowledge and his imaginative power must be formidable. He must have acquired the craftsmanship of the conductor, and he must possess inventive genius in addition.

If one considers the scholarship which is necessary for composing, the work of the juvenile or child composer appears as a truly miraculous manifestation of human gifts. It is far more impressive and much more important a phenomenon than that of the infant-prodigy conductor. In its most glorious instance, all the knowledge, the learning, and even the necessary experience seems to have been given by providence to the child Mozart—most likely the truest genius mankind has ever produced.

Almost all composers are *competent* conductors. Many composers have been, and are, *great* conductors. Originally, the composer was always his own conductor, but few composer-conductors now restrict themselves to conducting their own work. The relationship between conducting and composing is a puzzling one. Does conducting stimulate composing, even if there is no spark of inventive genius? Or does the permanent familiarity with great works of music stunt the ability to compose, and make the conductor write what the Germans abusively term Kapellmeistermusik—conductor's music?

Great composers are a rare phenomenon, and their gifts are not often recognized by their contemporaries—the old rule, that music can only be easily understood and appreciated when it is a hundred years old, acts against them.

With few exceptions, the treatment which mankind has meted out to its great composers can only be described as horrible.

No oily enunciations at the opening of Salzburg Festivals will eradicate the burning stigma of shame over the way Mozart was treated by the worthies of that very town. After a brief spell of security as member of the Archbishop's household, he, the 'villain and low fellow', the 'vile wretch', was, on the Archbishop's orders, bodily kicked out by the Archbishop's marshall.

Ten years later, when Mozart died in unrelieved pain and dismal poverty, his funeral was one of severe economy.* The few friends who accompanied the coffin did not even follow it to the common pit for dead paupers into which his body was thrown, because it was raining and windy. When Vienna's

---

* According to G. P. Clein, Mozart died of uraemia as the result of kidney diseases of long standing. Its symptoms can explain Mozart's belief that he was being poisoned, the mysterious visitor of the Requiem, and the terminal twitching, interpreted as an attempt to express the drum passage of the the Requiem with his mouth. (*Mozart—a study in renal pathology*, Kings College Gazette, 1968, 37.)

famous anatomist Hyrtl later tried to identify Mozart's skull, he had to choose from among many hundreds. The skull he eventually identified as Mozart's was probably someone else's.

If the shameful treatment of Mozart would have been an isolated incident, mankind could perhaps be forgiven. However few of those composers whose mock-art plaster busts are now a profitable side-line of the music shop, and adorn countless suburban mantelpieces the world over, have fared much better.

J. S. Bach was recognized as a very competent musician by his contemporaries—and yet had to earn his sustenance by teaching Latin to schoolboys, an activity which he strongly disliked. When he dared to complain that his application for a conductor's post had been unfairly rejected, he was put into prison for a month. Ten years after his death, his widow died in the Leipzig workhouse.

Mozart's cousin Weber* was one of the more fortunate ones: he lived to read that the first performance of *Der Freischütz* in 1821 was considered 'one of the most important events in German operatic history'. The financial rewards of this glory were, however, so poor that, suffering from severe pulmonary tuberculosis, which had caused repeated haemorrhages, he felt compelled to accept a conducting engagement in London. He needed desperately the fees he was to receive for the performances of *Oberon*, in order to prevent his wife and children from going hungry. Wretched and alone, he died in London in 1826.

Schubert perished in penury, misery and utter loneliness at the age of 31, as the result of typhoid fever, and no one seems to have visited him during the last ten days of his life. Towards the end of his life he learnt that his admired Goethe thought nothing of the music he had written for his poems. The Viennese people even spread the mischievous tale that Beethoven, too, thought that Schubert's songs were poor stuff. Schindler, Beethoven's secretary, later corrected this story and stated that

---

* Cousin by marriage: Weber's father was the brother of Mozart's wife's father.

during his last illness Beethoven's only pleasure had been the reading of Schubert's songs.

Few people were as badly exploited, neglected, and robbed by their friends as Schubert was. Contrary to widespread belief, Schwind's* famous drawing of *Schubert among his friends and admirers* is a sentimental reconstruction, and was painted many years after Schubert's death. For reasons of shameful personal envy, his great C major Symphony was deliberately concealed and was only accidentally discovered by Schumann in 1838, ten years after Schubert's death. The Unfinished Symphony, probably the most widely known symphonic work in the world, was hidden by his jealous 'friend' Hüttenbrenner for 37 years (until 1865). The work which Schubert regarded as his best, the 'Gasteiner' Symphony, was stolen and probably destroyed.

The catalogue of shame could be continued at length, and it is not *only* the public and the critics who behaved discreditably. Bruckner's Second Symphony was rejected as 'unplayable' by the Vienna Philharmonic Orchestra. When his Third ('Wagner') Symphony was eventually performed for the first time, all but ten people left the concert hall before the finale, in protest against that terrible noise.

Is there any redeeming feature in these accounts of incomprehension, of neglect and of outright cruelty?

Perhaps there is.

Sad as it may seem, despair, disillusion and suffering have proved to be important catalysts in all fields of artistic endeavour. Artists in financial distress, artists in hunger, artists suffering the pangs of unrequited love, have often written better poetry and music than when they enjoyed peace of mind; the phenomenon of the 'contrary effect' is not restricted to musical instruments alone. (See p. 54.)

---

* Moritz von Schwind (1804-1871) was a famous Austrian painter. In 1859 he designed the windows of Glasgow Cathedral.

Valid proof for this contention is produced by Mascagni's life. At the age of twenty-four years, he absconded from his musical college. This was an ill-considered step, which seemed to bar him from the further education necessary for the career he wished to pursue. His subsequent vagabond's life with an itinerant operetta company made a return to serious music even less feasible. An association with a young singer who bore him an illegitimate son complicated his private life, and the death of the child deepened his gloom. His angry father could not be approached for help. An indiscretion led to police searches, from which he had to hide under difficulties. Living on the miserable salary of a municipal music teacher in a small town, he composed a score which became one of the greatest successes in operatic history. Overnight, the young man of 26 became rich and famous, and all financial worries disappeared for the rest of his life. In security and tranquillity he composed another fifteen operas. One of them, *Le Maschere* (1901) was given the never-repeated publicity of seven simultaneous first nights in Italy's seven best-known opera houses, and Caruso sang, and Toscanini conducted its performance at La Scala. In spite of all this, *Cavalleria Rusticana*, the opera he had written in despair and poverty, remained his best work.

Peter Grimes, too, the most outstanding work of contemporary operatic history, can be quoted as an example. Written at the beginning of the last war, in half chosen, half enforced exile, most probably in despair and disappointment with a world which was about to drive out the devil—whom he hated —with the Beelzebub he could not accept, it brought its author universal fame and recognition. None of Britten's other operas has yet surpassed this supreme achievement.

Should we then, after all, be grateful to Salzburg's unchristian Archbishop? Might we now be without *Don Giovanni* and the other operas of Mozart's late period if a cleric had behaved decently, and allowed Mozart to remain, in security, a member of his household?

In a material sense, the general attitude to the creative artist has, no doubt, improved in our own period. To maintain life is for the artist now easier than it was, and at long last mankind has become aware of its responsibilities in this respect.

However, the fact that it is now easier to survive, and that there is no more need to go hungry is not the only criterion. Music can never remain static. It is in the very nature of Art that it must always strive for new means of expression. If music is to live, modern music has to be written, and there can be no return to old techniques and conceptions.

This does not need to diminish our love for our musical heritage, nor our duty and our desire to preserve it. On the contrary, caring for modern music helps in its own way the understanding of all music. Rightly we blame our forebears for their failure to respond intelligently to 'the new' in art. We feel rather superior when we learn that Bellini was advised to abandon that ultra-modern Parisian style which he had employed for *I Puritani*, and in unjustified righteousness we feel that if only Richard Wagner would write *now*, we would all welcome his work with joy.

However, modern music is on the whole still rejected and, as always, few are willing to make that special effort which is invariably necessary to understand new art.

Has our attitude to the composer of music really changed?

We deplore the conduct of the people of the past who failed to notice the great master, but may well do the same to the genius of our own time. Let us at least hope that this neglect is not entirely negative, and that its bitter cup acts as a spur to inspiration and creation!

EIGHTH CHAPTER

THE LIBRETTO
AND THE PUBLIC

THE LIBRETTO AND THE PUBLIC

It is often argued that opera is a dead art, a type of artistic achievement which has had its day. It is also said that opera houses depend for their revenue on those who know little about opera: those who *do* know about it do not pay for their seats. The bon mot contains a modicum of truth, but is obviously unfair to the large public who frequent opera houses, and whose enthusiasm refutes such arguments. All must be well as long as people love to hear opera performed and are prepared not only to pay extraordinarily high prices, but even to endure hardship. In order to witness exceptionally notable occasions, enthusiasts will camp in the street during a cold winter's night and wait patiently for the box office to open.

The number of great operatic works which are being written may well have declined. During the 1880s and 1890s several operas were written each year which became lasting additions to our operatic treasure house: for the last forty years or so, only about one work per decade has made the grade. However this does not really matter. Such fluctuations occur in all fields of artistic endeavour and opera will continue for as long as there is a public which loves these fascinating musical presentations: it is the attitude of the public, and not the influx of new works, which guarantees its continuance.

It is again the attitude of the public which warrants the indispensable financial support from private sources and public authorities. It does not matter that opera may well be an unreasonable or irrational blend of what is best in symphonic and vocal music, together with good or bad theatre, and with splendid or ridiculous pageantry. What *does* matter is to win the hearts of the coming generation, and to keep the public interested and satisfied.

It is easy to express such ideas in general terms. It is not so easy to come to valid conclusions as to the best policies to be pursued for such ends.

For most people, the enjoyment of opera consists in re-cognizing familiar music. It is obvious that this implies fairly close previous acquaintance with it. People who combine out-standing musical gifts with thorough musical training are exempted from this rule: a conductor, for example, may derive sensory acoustic pleasure from looking at, or reading, a score which he has never heard performed.

Most opera-goers are rather unlikely to enjoy an opera fully when they hear it for the first time. It may be a fascinating experience for them, and they may find the music attractive, but only increasing familiarity with it will bring full enjoyment. The maxim that one can only *really* enjoy an opera after one has heard it ten times contains a good deal of truth: the pleasantly anticipated and promptly fulfilled musical expectation forms the very basis of our enjoyment. Only the first few performances of a long opera may seem to last a long time. The better we know it, the more quickly time passes, and when we have come to love and understand it, the performance finishes far too soon.

In order to become familiar with an opera, we must be able fully to participate in its action as well as in its music. The words form an integral part of the action: we must not only musically, but also literally understand what is going on. This points to one of the dilemmas of opera. Should opera be sung in its original language or in the vernacular? The problem, for a long time hotly disputed by real and imagined experts, has recently solved itself, and practical considerations have settled the issue.

Opera is an international art, and those singers who are so famous that they are asked to perform all over the world are no longer prepared to learn the rôles in their repertoire in several languages: exceptions exist, and will continue to exist—a tenor of Hungarian origin can sing Radames in seven languages—but they are becoming rare, and artists in international demand generally insist on singing in the libretto's original language. This is sensible enough. Not only does it eliminate the strain of having to memorize the libretto in several languages, but it also ensures linguistically uniform performances. From Tokyo to Barcelona there is now this uniformity in most operas in international repertory, although the work may be performed by artists who have been thrown together by the dice of the opera planners, and the casting been further modified by the notorious exigencies of last-minute changes.

Some may well not approve of this solution, but no one can doubt that the problem is in fact solved, and that at least on the level on which international casting is practised, performance in the original language has become the established rule.

However, no sooner was this new uniformity established than unforeseen disturbances arose and began to complicate the issue. A brilliant Canadian soprano, an exciting mezzo-soprano from Bulgaria, a Viennese tenor and a famous Australian bass combine under the baton of a fashionable and competent conductor to perform an Italian opera. It is all very well sung, and results in a far more than adequate performance, and yet it does not quite sound as Italian opera should sound.

What went wrong?

The overtones were wrong.

Every language produces a characteristic sound, and the special character of this sound is due to the overtones which are emitted in the articulation of its words. These overtones are so highly characteristic that they enable us to tell at once that a group of people at a near-by table in the restaurant are speaking French, although they are so far away, or their voices so dimmed by the general hubbub, that we are unable to understand one word they say; they are so characteristic that we realize that people are speaking in Hungarian or in Finnish, even though we may not know a single word of these languages.

Overtones are an undetachable part of the 'tune' of language, and when we change our language, or learn a new one, after the overtones of our original language have already been firmly established in our speech—the critical age for this event is probably the seventh or eighth year—the overtones of our original language persist very tenaciously, and form an 'accent'. *'Accent' is therefore the transfer of overtones which belong to a different language, or to different regions or social groups within the same language-area, into a sound-picture in which such overtones are unusual.*

What frequently prevents perfection in phonetic singing is the fact that in spite of great efforts at proper enunciation the *natural* overtones may be missing. These natural overtones cannot be readily acquired at all, and can only be produced under the same exceptional circumstances under which a foreign accent can be almost completely concealed or eliminated.

As the result of international casting, two laws which are at times incompatible, are now emerging. The first is that the libretto's words will always sound best in the language in which it was written. Not less important, however, is the second law, i.e. that most singers will sound best if they sing in their own language. Phonetic singing is an attempt to achieve the almost impossible: the forming of overtones which can only be sounded under exceptional circumstances.

The reasons for the need to respect the overtones are not difficult to understand for those who are familiar with the texture of symphonic music. Every musical note is physically precisely determined, and will yet sound very differently when produced by a trumpet, by a violin, or by the piano. Only the overtones cause this difference. Among orchestral instruments the flute has the fewest overtones, which explains its rather spiritless sound in parts of its range. The instrument richest in overtones is the cello. If we eliminate the overtones altogether, we are left with the correctly pitched, but insipid sound of the audiometer.

In England, where the repertory of opera written in the native language is severely limited, opera, at least on international level is ideally cast with as many original, or almost accent-free voices as possible. This ensures that the resulting sound-picture, or the sound-colour of the words, is as it was originally intended. There is, however, another aspect to consider as well. The abundance of promising young singers which characterizes the present generation, makes it desirable that they should be heard under the best possible circumstances—and they will sound their best when they sing in English.

It is often argued that English is less singable than other languages, but this is quite untrue. What *is* true, and possibly the basis of such complaints, is that it is seemingly more difficult to combine English words with a vocal line than words of some other languages. However, one only needs to look at the vocal scores of Händel's English works to realize that the job can be done to perfection.

On a *national* level it is, therefore, essential to continue with opera in English. This does not need to be a 'second-best' type of arrangement. On the contrary, it fits in perfectly with the need to provide for that large section of the public who are unfamiliar with the original language, the opportunity to acquaint themselves with the details of the action, and the psychology of the opera's characters.

How much the pleasure of opera-going is increased by understanding all the words of a clearly sung libretto is known to everyone who has experienced it. For this reason, and in order to achieve true audience participation, Gustav Mahler recommended the translation of libretti.

Reflection, therefore, shows that there is no dilemma at all. We need both types of opera. On the international level, opera in in its original language has no doubt come to stay. On national level, better translations and attention to good enunciation are essential needs.

Unfortunately, the translating of operatic libretti is a difficult task, and the translation from the language which provides most libretti is, for linguistic reasons, particularly difficult: Italian will not blend readily into English. French occupies a middle position while German and English are fairly readily interchangeable, a fact which produced the American phenomenon of the 'schönst language'.*

All translations of libretti face the problem of adapting word-stress to existing music. Word-stress is a specific accentuation which has nothing to do with pronunciation or 'timbre' accent. It is strongly influenced by habit, and word accentuation can vary significantly in different regions which belong to the same language. For Irish ears, for instance, an accented third-last syllable is anathema, and therefore one does not buy one's stamps at the póstoffice, but at the postóffice. Irish doctors and nurses still prefer, even after many years of residence in England, the sterilízer, to the stérilizer, and do not even refrain from occasional distortions, as in the casu-álity department, rather than placing the accent too far forward for their liking.

The English, too, have some similar and perhaps even less consistent accent habits, particularly in expressions originating from foreign languages. A French college in London which, by every rule of the French language should be called the lycée, is so persistently referred to as the lýcée, that many French people believe that lýcée is the English word for lycée. If one would, however, conclude from the lýcée that the English always prefer to accentuate the first syllable, one need only refer to Caprí,

---

* At the end of the 19th century, the demands of a rapidly expanding American beer industry caused a considerable number of German brewery staff to immigrate to Milwaukee. Twenty years later, the schönst language had established itself: a newspaper was published and a number of books appeared, among them poetry. No corresponding mixture between English and either Italian or French seems possible. Quoted from memory, the poem *The Greenhorn* (New Immigrant) began:

> A greenhorn kennst Du by sy shoe
> that must I Dir erklären.
> I wonder how sie stande do
> such tighte boots to wearen!

and the last lines of *Faust* were:

> The Glocke rings, and with Gebimmel
> Ascendet she up to the Himmel.

which should of course always be called Cápri, to realize that this is not the case.

No one can deny the British, or any other nation's sovereign right to pronounce any word as they may wish. It may, however, be opportune to point out that this habit can prove extraordinarily irritating to foreigners, a fact which is almost totally unsuspected by the British. A French journalist, for instance, once wrote* that the English pronunciation of 'Renáysance' for Renaissánce is so irritating to French ears that it produces a shudder of dislike of the English. Most French people are prepared to admit that this, while journalistically exaggerated, is basically true.

In spite of recent strides to improve the pronunciation of musical terms, the announcers of the B.B.C. still prefer the works of Chópin to those of Chopín, and cling grimly with rare exceptions to the horrible Debússy for Debussy.

Music critics too are grave offenders. No one can reasonably expect a critic of singing to be able to sing, but we are entitled to expect good standards in their own pronunciation from those who adjudicate the pronunciation of French in singing. When broadcasting, for instance, they should not refer to Bízet instead of Bizét.

It is said that Smétana was so disconcerted by persistent mispronunciation of his name by Anglo-Saxon friends, that he referred to Beethoven's Eighth Symphony as a mnemonic device:

you must call me Sme-ta-na Sme-ta-na Sme-ta-na you must call me

Sme-ta-na Sme-ta-na Sme-ta-na not Sme-ta-na not Sme-ta-na

---

* It is regretted that no exact citation can be given for this quotation from a Paris newspaper of 1947 or 1948.

Many Czech words are subject to a syllable-stress which sounds odd to non-Slavs. However, respecting it is rewarding, as it is the clue to the syncopation in Czech popular music, which was so often utilized by Smetana and Dvořák. The proper pronunciation of the female form of this latter name, for instance, is Dvorákova and not Dvorakóva, which makes this Czech name appear to be Polish. Janáček was linked with Bŕno (or Brünn in the Austrian tradition), but not with the B.B.C.'s Brnó. *Mr. Brouček* from brouk, i.e. beetle, with a diminutive -ček, 'Mr. Smallbeetle' should be pronounced with the o as in 'brogue'.

The name of the Hungarian composer F. Lehár, too, is almost invariably mispronounced. The accent on the 'á' does *not* mean that the stress falls on the second syllable; every single Hungarian word, without exception, carries the tonic stress on its first syllable. The accent only indicates that the 'á' should be pronounced as in 'bar'; without the accent, the composer's name would become 'Lehor'.

Accomplished translations of operatic libretti are certainly desirable, but it is as well to remember that true perfection in the blending of word and music can never be achieved. Even in the original language many libretti occasionally affront every rule of word-melody and declamation. *Die Zauberflöte* contains a well-known example, in which the word *noch* is quite wrongly placed, a fault which can only be explained by Mozart's avowed contention that poetry must, under all conditions, remain the music's servant.

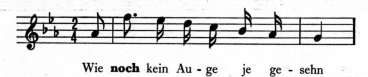

Wie **noch** kein Au - ge   je   ge - sehn

Weber, who did not share this view, has emphasized the need for correct word accent. Nevertheless, in one of his most perfect melodies he committed a grave offence against his own principle.

Durch   die Wäl - **der** durch   die   Au - en

Such maladaptations can be found in Italian opera as well. Notwithstanding Verdi's famous punctiliousness in such matters, one example has crept into *Un Ballo In Maschera:*

Vol - - ta   la   ter - re - **a**   fron - te alle   stel - le

and it is not surprising that Cavaradossi's crime against the pronunciation of the past participle of *amare* (*amato*)—

E non ho   a- ma-**to**   mai tan - to   la   vi - ta,

—swiftly leads to his execution by firing-squad.

In the most famous aria of French opera, Don José in vain tries to move his recalcitrant Carmen's heart. Would his 'O'-level examiner have shown more mercy? The French for 'flower' is *la fleur*, with the emphasis on '*fleur*', not—

La   fleur   que   tu   m'a - vais   je - té   -   e,

and to make matters worse, the next few bars contain three wong *accents toniques* in '*m'était*', in '*flétrie*', and particularly in '*séche*'.

dans   ma   pri - son,   **m'é** tait   res - té - e,   **flé -**

trie   et   se - **che**   cet - te   fleur.

These examples in no way imply criticism of Mozart, Verdi or the other composers. They are only given in order to encourage the would-be translator, and to console him if he is unable to avoid the occasional wrong word-accent in fitting his translation to the music.

It is difficult to commission a good translation. At its best level, translating is a labour of love, and a single word alone can cost a night's sleep. All the more important to encourage the amateur would-be translators!

A factor which considerably complicates translating, and which is often overlooked, is the aim at assonance, the matching of the vowels, which characterizes the Italian libretto. In singing together, the characters use different words, and often express differing emotions—but, as far as they can, they will do so by using corresponding vowels.

Many examples could be given: the one on the opposite page is from the final scene of Don Giovanni, just prior to the entry of the Commendatore.

Donna Elvira's *iniquità* blends perfectly with Don Giovanni's *umanità* and Leporello's *cor non hà*.

The English translation (by Edward Dent) achieves assonance (Donna Elvira: *just as you are*, Don Giovanni: *follow their star*, Leporello: *that shows no scar*) but only at the price of a very

free rendering and by putting a statement into Leporello's mouth which can only make sense as a report on Don Giovanni's electrocardiogram.

The German translation (Breitkop & Härtel edition) keeps somewhat nearer to the original meaning but it can be appreciated how the sound picture of the final note must change if the uniform 'a' vowel in the Italian is replaced by a mixture of *Pfuhl*, *Welt* and *Stein*.

Translations do not last forever. The reason for their evanescence is probably that good writing is an art. The original libretto, if it is a work of art, remains, like all true art does, forever 'timeless'. Translating is not art: it is expert craftsmanship. It is craftsmanship of a difficult type, but still essentially a craft and not art, and therefore echoes its own period. Translations are, for this reason, liable to 'date', and new translations become necessary from time to time. This need arises whenever the character of the living language has sufficiently changed to expose modes of expression as *dated*, which occurs every forty or fifty years. This greatly complicates the whole issue of the translations, but may well be a blessing in disguise, as it forces us to attempt new and better translations.

Occasionally a translation achieves the almost impossible it can, at least in some passages if not *in toto*, be an improvement on the original. Such paradoxical effects can arise under varying circumstances.

(1) Libretto writers can yield to the temptation to let their characters speak in an artificial language, which, so they believe, fits the period of the plot. It is very doubtful whether this artifice has ever been fully successful. The invented language of the past almost invariably sounds contrived and artificial. A plain and straightforward translation of a contrived libretto may remove its mannerisms, and can therefore give a better all-round effect. This is, with some justification, claimed for Allan Pryce-Jones' translation of *Der Rosenkavalier*, though it must be admitted that by eliminating the artificiality of Hoffmansthal's mock 18th century phrasing, its charm—if a synthetic one—is lost as well.

(2)   A translated phrase may fit the musical passage better than the original one. The placing of the word 'champagne' in the 'champagne' ensemble of Christopher Hassall's translation of *Die Fledermaus* is a good example

Deutscher Sekt?

ju - belnd   wird   Cham - **pag** - ner

Good, dry Champagne!

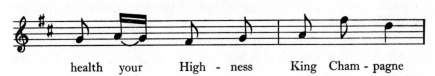

health   your   High - ness   King   Cham - pagne

(3)   Wagner's musical genius remained for a long time insufficiently recognized. His importance as renovator of German thought and language on the basis of middle-German and of Schopenhauer was on the other hand much overrated. A plain English translation can eliminate pompous phraseology, and it is feasible that this contributed to the recent successes of Wagner operas sung in English.

The English translation of one particular passage may have even been diplomatically helpful. Hans Sach's musically beautiful, yet historically unjustified and rather offensive remark about the intrusion of Italian humbug and trumpery* into German lands, is in its English translation generally rendered as an invasion by 'foreign mists.' Since the end of the war, some Ger-

---

* waelscher Dunst und waelscher Tand.

man theatres are said to have adopted the English suggestion and have replaced the word *waelsch* (Italian) by *fremd* (foreign).

If one does not know any better, and if the musical passage is beautiful, it is quite possible to become attached to the words of a bad translation. *Don Giovanni* was for 150 years in Germany and in Austria almost always sung in German. This explains the popularity of the horrible: 'Reich mir die Hand, mein Leben' (give me the hand, my life), which in Germany is considered more beautiful and poetic than 'Là ci darem la mano.'

Some translations reveal odd discrepancies. Radames discloses that the route which his soldiers will take goes through 'the gorges of Napata, *le gole di Napata*'. In the French performances of Aida they intend to march over 'the pass of Ténapa, *le col de Ténapa*'. It has, so far, not been possible to trace how this disparity arose, and whether either of the two places are named in Mariette's sketch.

Libretto writing always carries its own problems, the main problem being that it embodies the obligation to serve *two* masters.

The first loyalty of the libretto writer must be towards the original source of the opera—whatever this source may be—in order to enable him to transfer a clear picture of the original contents into the new work.

We are inclined to think of opera almost entirely in terms of its music, and to regard the action as an unimportant framework or 'vehicle' for the music. This makes us forget how significantly and greatly the choice of the operatic subject loomed in the past over the composer's horizon. It was widely believed, particularly by the Italian composers of the 19th century, that the *libretto* was the decisive factor for the success or failure of their work, and this view was reflected in the choice of operatic subjects: infinite pains were taken to choose a suitable plot, and to express it in appropriate words.

For a long time, the *conditio sine qua non* for success in Italian opera seemed to be that its plot had been a success on the Paris stage (even Shakespeare's plays were sometimes seen in this light), or, at least, a success in French literature.

In order to give a few examples from a multitude, one can refer to Donizetti's, *Elisir d'amore* based on Eugene Scribe's play *Le Philtre*, to Verdi's *Rigoletto*—from Victor Hugo's play *Le Roi s'amuse* and to Puccini's *Tosca*—from Victorien Sardou's play *La Tosca*.

In English, in German and in French, one *adapts* a play or book to a libretto. In Italy rather more aptly, one *reduces* a work to a libretto. This usage explains the term: the *libretto*, i.e. the *little* book, is a diminutive of the *libro*, i.e. *the book*, and generally contains far fewer words.

The first person who attempted to lay down rules for the construction of a libretto was the Italo-Austrian aristocrat Andrea Maffei (1798-1885), who used his thorough knowledge of English and German to acquaint Italy with previously not translated works (he was the translator of Milton's *Paradiso perduto*, as well as of Heine's *Guglielmo Ratcliff* which inspired the young Mascagni to the opera of that name).

His intimate friendship with Verdi made Andrea Maffei take an interest in the operatic libretto, and he adapted Schiller's drama *Die Räuber* to the libretto of *I Masnadieri**. In a foreword to this opera, Maffei elaborated the theory of the 'concave lens structure' of the libretto. Ideally, a libretto *should retain all the characteristics as well as all the significant contents of the original, but it must render them as if seen through a reducing lens, i.e. without a change in their 'essential physiognomy'*. This theory so appealed to Verdi that when he commissioned Piave to adapt Carcano's *Macbeth* translation for opera (Verdi read Shakespeare, his favourite dramatic source, always in the Carcano† translation), Maffei was asked to supervise the fidelity of the transcription.

---

* The only opera of Verdi's which had its première in London, in 1847.

† Giulio Carcano (1821-82) converted the Shakesparian drama's blank verse (iambic pentameter, and essentially endecasyllabic) with the "indefatigable tenacity which characterizes the people of Lombardy" into Italian hendeca-syllables.

The resulting Macbeth libretto is the perfect example of the reducing theory. In some 3,250 words it contains a surprising proportion of the contents of Shakespeare's play of 16,700 words, thus showing a 'reduction index' of approximately one in five, a proportion which is fairly constant. Sardou's *La Tosca* contains 17,127 words to Giacosa's and Illica's *Tosca* of 3,720 (reduction index 1:4.6), and Victor Hugo's *Le Roi s'amuse* contains 16,800 words to Piave's *Rigoletto* 4,100 (1:4).

The second master which the libretto wrier hast to serve, is, of course, the composer. Examination of the circumstances under which the libretto writers had to carry out their tasks, not only makes it understandable that so many poetically and dramatically poor libretti exist, but makes it in fact surprising that there exist so many good, or partially good ones. Some libretti are indeed excellent, and even bereft of Mozart's divine music, Lorenzo da Ponte's *Le Nozze di Figaro* makes delightful reading.

Writing for operatic singing must, of course, fulfil special and individual requirements, and cannot be judged by the general standards applied to literature and poetry. Composers have often tried to impose such tyrannical impositions on their libretto writers that it is not surprising that few writers of acknowledged literary merit found the task tempting. Verdi was one of the most exacting composers in this respect, and subdued a record number of libretto writers. Arrigo Boito had to 'subjugate his own genius to Verdi's genius willingly and completely', and it was said that the only libretto writer Verdi did not drive to distraction was Tommaso de Celano!* Of course, writers cannot readily submit to such demands without damaging the quality of their own writing and, by and large, libretto writing became a hack job.

---

* Tommaso de Celano (who died in 1253), is reputed to be the author of the celebrated triple verses of the Requiem:

> Dies irae, dies illa
> Solvet saeclum in favilla
> Teste David cum Sibylla . . . etc.

Although many operatic libretti of the first half of the 19th century are derived from Shakespeare's tragedies or from Victor Hugo's dramas, they have stylistically nothing in common with their sources. Their style derives from the ballads and romances of Giovanni Berchet (1783-1851)* and Luigi Carrer (1801-1850), and later, towards the end of the century, the influence of Carducci's poetry made itself felt as well.

The libretto writer's rewards were moderate, and in Verdi's time the rate generally was 100 lire per act. The contractual relationship between the composer and the creator of the 'original source' was ill-defined, and not infrequently subject to strain.

It is to the credit of a French professional body, the Société des Auteurs, Compositeurs et Editeurs de Musique, that they laid down fair rules for the division of royalties, and these French rules were accepted by the Italian courts in the famous case which Giovanni Verga brought against Mascagni and the publisher Sonzogno, on account of their unauthorized use of Verga's play *Cavalleria Rusticana* for a libretto.

The French rules laid down that the author of the 'original source' must invariably be regarded as co-author of the opera; that the composer should receive 50% of the royalties; and that the original author should share with the libretto writer the other 50% in the proportion of 25% each.

Of course, this was only relevant in a comparatively small number of cases: it is easy to forget that the successful operas form only a minute minority among the estimated hundred thousand operas which failed to bring success to their authors.

The manner in which we express our appreciation and gratitude to those who give us pleasure in a performance is a rather odd one: to applaud is basically a crude and uncivilised activity, ill-fitted to follow (and even more ill-fitted to blot out), the final chords of beautiful music. It is significant that in its Roman origins (it first appears in Cicero) the word *adplaudo or adplodo*, refers to the approval of political speeches.

---

* Giovanni Berchet lived as a political refugee from 1821-1848 in London.

In the performing arts, applause has become the accepted means of acknowledgement, because in its various forms of clapping of hands, stamping of feet, shouting, and whistling, it seems the only sign of immediate approval mankind is capable of. It is certainly regrettable that no more dignified form of approval has ever been found practicable.

For the public, it is an active release of energy after a prolonged period of physically inactive concentration. For the artist it is the expression of that reward which all reproducing artists long for, the token of approval from their fellow human beings. Their desire for success and approbation (though this desire is occasionally denied in honest conviction, while other artists, less convincingly, pretend that they do not give a damn), conforms to a deep-seated trait of human psychology.

On the whole, applause is taken more seriously than it deserves. It has even been suggested that the intensity of the applause is in direct proportion to the loudness of the final chord, and that this has contributed to the tendency to end musical compositions with a fortissimo chord. One can only hope that this allegation of calculated subservience by composers is a wrong one.

Applause lends itself to abuse, and has therefore great potential nuisance value. There is no doubt that the concert-hall public has made greater progress towards good taste in applauding than the public of the opera houses. The old, disturbing custom of applauding during pauses between movements of a symphonic work has now been eradicated. At concerts, one can now generally hear the final bars of the performed work, and the sound of the closing passages is no longer drowned by ill-timed noise. It was not always so. Applause after difficult or impressive passages during concertos for solo instruments was the rule rather than the exception until not very many years ago.

Why the operatic public should have been left so far behind in the progress towards good musical behaviour is difficult to decide. Why should Puccini's arias serve as a signal for noisy eruptions? It can hardly be a desire to hear the same aria twice for the same money, as repetitions are now exceedingly rare, and are generally discouraged.

It may well be true that after a well-sung aria artists expect applause, and that without it they might feel so disappointed that it could pejoratively influence their subsequent singing. However, if no applause during acts were ever forthcoming, artists would soon lose their feeling of disappointment and would expect their 'reward' only at the end of the act. The public's memory should surely be long enough to remember exceptionally well-sung passages when the curtain falls!

Elimination of applause during acts would also have the indirect effect of preventing the manifestation of claques. All attempts at exaggerated ovations during performances, whether by well-meaning friends or possibly by hired hands, are apt to irritate the public. Britain's opera houses have been fortunate in that no claque has ever been able to establish itself firmly. In other countries, these claques are a nuisance to the public and in the long run to the artists as well. Some 'humoristic' music books have surrounded the claques with a halo they ill deserve. To approach singers with the offer of such services is a form of blackmail: an artist's justified reluctance to hire and pay carries the risk of 'boos' and other nastiness. The stories of the poor, highly gifted young music students who form themselves into a claque in order to hear opera performed without having to pay for their tickets, are fairy-tales and the claques are nothing but rackets.

Another bad habit which cries out for change, is the timing of applause at the end of an act or at the end of a performance.

When Richard Strauss was Director of the Vienna Opera, he particularly requested his public not to applaud too soon. He was very anxious that this unwritten law should be strictly respected. The public became so keen on this essentially praise-worthy ritual that they were apt to overdo their abstention: at the fall of the curtain there would be no applause whatsoever until the very last sound had completely, utterly and totally ceased to vibrate. This restraint once caused Strauss considerable embarrassment. During the short moment of absolute silence at the end of the first act of *Lohengrin*, Mrs. Strauss' voice could be plainly heard addressing her escort in the director's box as follows: "I can only say that this sounded different when I used to sing it."*

Apart from being disturbing, premature applause is amateurish as well; lacking respect for the duration of sounds is the hallmark of the inexperienced.

Such comment, however, should not be taken as disparagement of amateur activities in music. On the contrary, amateur activities are not only important for music, they are also one of the most rewarding activities life has to offer.

The division of music into groups of music *listeners* and of music *makers*, with the creation of a musical aristocracy, is against music's best interests. The tripartite division into music creators, music performers and listeners is even more artificial. Any barrier dividing the music maker from the dilettante is not only unwelcome, but also contrary to the lessons which can be learnt from the history of music.

Every one of Beethoven's symphonies was first performed by orchestras which had to rely to a substantial extent on amateur instrumentalists. Many of the early Italian, particularly Venetian, composers, were dilettanti.† Only as the result of increasing technical perfection, and the acceptance of the virtuoso principle, did, towards the middle of the 19th century, the trained professional musician oust the amateur from the concert platform and the orchestra pit.

Before the invention of the gramophone, operatic music

---

* Mrs. Strauss, Pauline de Ahna, was before her marriage a professional singer. The role of Elsa at the performance mentioned above was sung by Maria Jeritza.
† Benedetto Marcello (1686-1739), Venetian composer and creator of the *Estro poetico-armonico*, called himself 'Nobile dilettante'.

was played at home from the piano score, while piano arrangements for four hands offered the most satisfactory method for
hearing symphonic music at home. Beethoven's secretary recommended the playing of Beethoven's symphonies in this way as an
easy and worthwhile task for every music lover. By the end of the
19th century, the organists had developed the art of transcription
with extraordinary detail.

Although the general need for individual music-making
was greater during the days when the 'musical box', the street
organ and the mechanical piano ('Pianola'), were the principal
forms of *mechanized music*, the *personal* need still persists un-
changed. It was not at all a bad feature of the century before the
First World War, that every person who claimed to be 'educated'
was expected to have had private tuition in music. Musical gifts,
even outstanding musical gifts, only manifest themselves during
actual instruction in music and there is evidence that such
talents can easily remain stunted if the instruction is not con-
tinuous, or not intensive enough. The introduction of music into
the ordinary school curriculum is a step in the right direction;
but class teaching, however useful it is, does not eliminate the
need for private tuition.

At the present time, gramophone records and radio replace
the four-handed piano arrangements. As the result of it all,
musical talent may well be left undeveloped because many gifted
young people only *listen* to music and do not feel the urge to
make it. Youth orchestras and other group activities which make
the playing of instruments appealing, are important for the
closing of this gap between performers and listeners, but the
success of these ventures is as yet rather limited, although everyone agrees that widespread, active music making is highly desirable.

It has already been mentioned that singing must not be
left to professional singers alone, but in a country where amateur
choirs enjoy such large membership and high standards, such
exhortations seem hardly necessary. Composing, too, should not
—and cannot—be left entirely to those of genius. Basic training in

harmony and counterpoint is not difficult to acquire. Any adult who has learnt to play an instrument, can by self-instruction with books, and with the help of a piano, acquire that technical knowledge which is necessary for simple composing quite readily during odd evenings. It is an enjoyable and calming pastime to compose a piece of instrumental music, or to set the words of a favourite piece of poetry (home-made for preference), to music. The feeling of accomplishment which can be experienced at its completion is surprisingly exhilarating, even if posterity will never want to know about it!

The point of enjoyment in playing an instrument arrives long before technical competence is reached. Technical competence, however desirable it may be, is not essential for the enjoyment of music making. To react as if a string quartet by Beethoven could come to permanent harm because a violin has played an F instead of an F sharp is unreasonable and objectionable. There is good evidence that composers very much desired the amateurs to *play* their works. Mozart has dedicated one of his most enchanting pieces of chamber music (B flat major, K.589) to an influential amateur cellist who, as he knew very well, could not play half of it. Most of Beethoven's piano, as well as his violin and piano sonatas, and even his string quartets, were not written for public performance *only*, but to be played at home and enjoyed.

The yardstoick of prfessional music-making is perfection. The yardstick for the amateur is the enjoyment. Enjoyment and enthusiasm should not be belittled, and many professional musicians like to associate with competent amateurs from time to time, in order to share sensations which can readily wither in the profession.

If we imagine *Musica* as an Olympian goddess, then the personal offering of a sonatina, scratched out on the fiddle in questionable intonation, is surely more pleasing to her than the mass-produced noise of the latest 'hi-fi' stereo gadget.

Good music, after all, always remains good music. Schön-berg's dictum that "good music is always instantaneously recognizable, even if it is scored for the zither",* could be continued with the words ". . . or badly played". Surely it is more important to play badly than not to play at all, particularly if bad playing is not a permanent feature, but acts as a stimulus to improvement.

If bad playing cannot destroy good music, *good* playing can, through the virtuosity and the rhythmic artistry of good musicians, ennoble even the most indifferent or trite entertainment stuff. In some respects, jazz musicians and popular singers are the virtuoso descendants of the gifted amateurs. Between them, jazz in the twenties and 'pop' in the sixties have revived the art of improvisation, in jazz terminology referred to as the 'break'. The joyfulness which jazz musicns brought into their playing has encouraged fraternity among musicians, and has contributed to the result that musicians have virtually overcome the problems which are due to differences in race, colour and religion.

The strict division between light (or entertainment) music and serious (or classical) music is a feature of the 19th century. A great deal of serious music was written with the sole object of entertaining, and still does its job quite superbly well! It has been suggested that the reception by the audience is the dividing factor between light and serious music, and that, for instance, Mozart's 'Eine kleine Nachtmusik' is a serious work when performed at a symphonic concert, but becomes entertainment when played at a garden fete.

---

* Schönberg's remark is often quoted in the above, somewhat inaccurate manner. As its correct version has never been recorded, Professor Egon Wellesz has advised its inclusion here. It requires the explanation that in colloquial Viennese—and Schönberg much enjoyed speaking in dialect—the zither was referred to as the 'Maurerklavier', the bricklayer's piano. In a conversation about the difference between trivial and good music, Schönberg said that the discriminating item about good music was that 'one recognizes it at once' "auch wann's es am Maurerklavier spüln" 'even if played on the bricky's piano' .Schönberg was fond of light music, especially Johann Strauss', though he disliked trivial music.

Several other theories have been put forward: entertainment music, it is contended, does not make the demands which serious music always makes, nor does it compel the listener to 'come to terms with it'. It just 'provides', or 'grants a request'. This 'providing' fulfils mankind's desire for 'mood makers' or 'mood models': gay music makes gay, sad music brings pensive thoughts, marches and dances stimulate collective feelings. All this the light music manages to achieve, even without penetrating into consciousness.

The popular arrangements and transcriptions of the 19th century, which became the fashion for the coffee-house and hotel orchestras, provoked and extended the division between light and serious music. The increasing demand for entertainment music stimulated its production, and this production has recently risen still further in response to the demands of radio, television and recording companies. Its present abundance makes the sorting of the wheat from the chaff more and more difficult.

Jazz aligned itself fundamentally with entertainment music, but its musical and rhythmical values were soon universally recognized. It seems fitting that the jazz idiom, which sprang originally from folk music alone, was introduced into opera by Gustav Mahler's son-in-law Ernest Krenek (in "*Jonny spielt auf* in 1927), because Mahler made prominent use of European folk tunes in his own symphonic and vocal music. The success of Křenek's experiment seemed to promise that the jazz idiom would be freely absorbed into serious music, but this has not happened yet. In 1931, a jazz opera, *Porgy and Bess*, with Negro Spirituals in a jazz context, again seemed to herald a new era, but nothing came of it. Perhaps it was due to Gershwin's early death that this work remained solitary, and the musical results which his link with Schönberg might have produced must remain guess-work.

Under certain circumstances, the opera-goer's innocent pleasure of listening to singing and music can assume an almost sinister aspect: it can become obsessive and lead to 'music addiction'. This is, fortunately, a rather rare condition. However, the present public preoccupation with addictions makes it desirable to look at this problem from a general point of view.

The normal human being is not prone to addictions. Contrary to widespread belief, neither friend nor pedlar easily cause him to become addicted, and the addiction to alcohol proves this point. Most people have, at one time or another, been tempted to drink too much. While this can well lead to trouble, to a charge of driving under the influence of drink, or even to a manslaughter charge, it does *not* necessarily lead to addiction.

In the case of alcohol, the pedlar is the socially very highly respected wine merchant, or the somewhat less respected licensee of the public house. If addiction occurred as easily as is claimed, the ubiquitous alcohol pedlar would be able to seduce everyone who can afford to buy alcohol into becoming an alcoholic.

This does *not* happen, because in a *normal* person powerful inhibitions against addiction form an effective protective mechanism. A well-balanced human being may be drunk once or twice, but he is immune to the danger of addiction: the toxic action of alcohol brings his inhibitions into play, and he learns to use alcohol as a stimulant without fear of becoming a chronic alcoholic.

Only those *do* become addicts whose inhibitions—as the result of a personality defect—are abnormal. It is the personality defect which causes the dependence and addiction, and not the availability of the poison.

The present craze of young people for a whole series of new poisons or drugs is not a craze for 'addiction': it is a sign of the incautious curiosity of the young, which is being aroused by reports or tales of new experiences. Only those people who are accompanied by a personality defect on their 'trip' proceed to addiction—usually with heroin. Despite a public belief to the contrary, this only occurs in a proportion similar to that of potential alcoholics among ordinary drinkers.

The underlying, probably genetically determined, personality defect produces an inability, or an unwillingness, to face certain realities of life. It emerges generally as an obsessional need for diversion, as a need for liberation from situations which are felt to be oppressive. The main action of alcohol, sleeping tablets, or drugs upon the addict is always that oblivion, that 'liberation', and the craving for them must be interpreted in this manner.

If someone enjoys music, he can listen for hours with rapt attention, and all worries and preoccupations are temporarily eliminated. It is quite obvious that this 'rapt attention' can form that very diversion from the vicious circle of thought for which the addiction-prone personality is always longing.

The visual element strengthens the 'diversion potential' and opera can therefore become addictive, or rather more correctly expressed, can become habit-forming. Every opera house is aware of these addicts, many of whom may have passed through other addictions. Their personality defects can make them a nuisance, particularly when they become obsessively linked to certain artists. Artists instinctively distinguish such people from their ordinary admirers. As long as they are able to buy their tickets, opera addicts are of course welcome at the box office. When the buying of tickets becomes a serious financial problem, the constant efforts to secure admission can become as persistent and objectionable as any other attempt to secure the object of a craving. Some music addicts like to pose as music experts, others have a genuine misconception regarding their own knowledge.

Almost every opera-goer is a self-appointed critic. If one could collect and record all the enormously different opinions which are expressed at the end of every performance, the results would be stupefying. The discussion of the performance among friends is no doubt an integral part of that enjoyment which stems from an evening at the opera. It is, however, surprising how many people find it enjoyable to criticize conductor, singer and performance with incredible acidity. The irony of it is that the same people may well have applauded most enthusiastically at the performance itself. Asked why they applauded what they later condemned as incompetent, they will often admit that they enjoyed the performance while it lasted—and equally enjoyed tearing it to pieces.

Many members of the public, even some of the better informed ones, have taken up the canard of the 'ruined voice' (see p. 110). Otherwise sensible people can be heard to proclaim the most astonishing piffle as to which commission or omission has caused the 'irretrievable' ruin of a singer's voice. Fortunately for the artist, generally all is well again in time for the next performance.

London's public is regarded by many artists as the most fair and agreeable audience in the whole world. It has also the reputation of being particularly generous to people who sing a rôle at short notice. Although, in general, Londoners expect the foreigner to speak English *well*, they will always give special praise to foreign singers who sing in English, however wrong their pronunciation may be. In Italy these reactions are reversed. Italians generally greet even the poorest attempt at speaking their language with over-generous praise. But if he *sings* in Italian, the foreigner meets a very different response. At the first substitution of a closed 'e' for an open 'e', or vice versa, he may induce shouting and whistling, as well as many other ill-mannered demonstrations, even if his voice is splendid, his fame world-wide and his singing musically perfect.

The success of many of the opera festivals which have recently emerged all over the world has encouraged opera lovers to travel abroad. Visits to opera houses abroad combine welcome change with an equally welcome recognition of familiar operatic surroundings and form most enjoyable holiday experiences. It may, therefore, be helpful to end this chapter with a list of some of those expressions relating to opera which are perfectly acceptable in England, but are 'howlers' abroad.

Cosey—this opera is really quite unknown beyond the English Channel. It is always referred to as *Così fan tuttè*, and necessarily so. The literal translation is *Thus do all women*, and it is as senseless to refer to an opera as '*Thus*' as it would be to refer to Shakespeare's comedy as 'Much'.

The Don is also unknown abroad. The effect which this expression produces, might be compared to that which the use of *The Sir* instead of *Falstaff* would make in England. The 'a' in *Don Giovanni* should be pronounced short, as in 'Annie', and not long as in 'Blarney'.

Cav and Pag aer only popular in England and America. To Italian ears, Cav and Pag sounds like 'a tail of straw' pronounced in a rustic dialect from northern Italy.

Forza is not an opera, but the crowd's call of encouragement for their football team. The opera is invariably referred to as *La Forza del Destino*, and its name cannot be abbreviated.

In German, *Die Frau* means *The Wife*, and remarkably enough, it means 'my own wife' for the exactly corresponding set for whom 'the wife' conveys this meaning in England. The opera itself must therefore be referred to as *Die Frau ohne Schatten* (or *Frau ohne Schatten*), with the stress on *Schatten* in order to make the crucial point, which is that it refers to a woman who lacks a shadow.

In conversation with Germans, it is best not to use the definite article preceding the name of a German opera, *even if one is speaking in English*. The English 'the' is not changeable, but in German the definite article must follow the rules of declension. It would therefore sound quite correct to say: "Unless *Die Walküre* is sung well, it is no pleasure to listen to it," because *Die Walküre* is the subject of the sentence and is phrased in the nominative. However, to say "Last week I saw a performance of *Die Walküre*" would sound wrong, because *Die Walküre* now requires the genitive case, which in English is 'of the', but in German just changes the 'Die' to 'Der'. Either this would now become "Last week I saw a performance of *Der Die Walküre*" which, though arguably correct, is ridiculous, because it repeats the definitive article in a quite unacceptable way, as in '*of the the Valkyrie*'—or it would become 'Last week I saw a performance of *Der Walküre*". This, too, sounds wrong in German, as it may well mean *of the Valkyrie*, but could also mean *The Valkyrie Man*.

Germans, Austrians and Swiss simply avoid the whole problem by never using the definite article where it may become liable to be affected by a declension. In speech as well as in print, the operas are therefore referred to as *Walküre*, as *Freischütz*, and as *Rheingold*, and the expressions '*Die Walküre*', '*Der Freischütz*' and '*Das Rheingold*' are only used when referring to the opera's title itself.

In Italian, too, the article in an opera's title can become a stumbling-block. When opera was developed in the 17th century, it was customary to use the article in the title. Therefore, '*L'Orfeo*' refers to an *opera*, but 'Orfeo' only to one of its characters just as '*Il Giasone*' does in relation to 'Giasone', or '*L'Arianna*'* in relation to 'Arianna' and so on. A recent revival of Monteverdi's *La Favola d'Orfeo* had its title contracted to '*Orfeo*': this was anachronistic and it should have been '*L'Orfeo*'.

Titles of this period are also dangerous because fashion then favoured mythological subjects with female names of Greek origin, some of which, by ending with '*o*', are exceptions to the general rule of Italian gender endings, in which '*o*' signifies masculine and '*a*' feminine†.

The unwary could easily assume that a character which is called 'Calisto' is male, and he would then refer to Cavalli's opera as '*Il Calisto*' instead of *La Calisto*. '*Il Calisto*' is, of course,

---

* L'Arianna is an only partially preserved work by Monteverdi (1567-1643). Il Giasone is by Cavalli (1602-1676).

† Other names belonging to this group are:
Clio, the Muse of history
Echo, the Nymph who, as a punishment was made to repeat the last syllable. As it was a nymph who gave the acoustic phenomenon its name and its explanation, Echo should even in English be of female gender. In Italy it would certainly have to be 'Miss Echo' and not 'Sir Echo';
Erato, the Muse of the poetry of love
Ero, Leander's unfortunate beloved
St. Eustochio, the daughter of Paola, a follower of St. Hieronymus
Io, who had to suffer transformation into a cow
Saffo, the Greek poetess of Lesbos
and Dido, Juno etc. Lohich become Didone and Junone in Italian.

a perfectly suitable title for an opera, though it would be desirable
to specify whether it refers to the ex-slave who was made Pope
Calisto I and became San Calisto (end of the 2nd century), or to
Calisto II (11th Century, 'Concordat of Worms') or to Calisto III
(born 1378).

It would also be quite correct to call an opera *Il Callista*—
provided the hero is a chiropodist by trade—or *La Callista*, in
the case of a lady chiropodist.

In England, Germany and America the Italian noun
'coloratura' is widely used to mean a special vocal quality—the
ability to sing high passages with agility. The decoration of notes
became necessary as the result of the cembalo's inability to *sustain*
a note, and passages repeating the note several times became
desirable. Such *fioriture* were accepted as an improvisation to
which artists were entitled, and which gave them the opportunity
to display special vocal agility. In Italian, however, 'coloratura'
is not used in a musical sense and simply means 'colouring';
only in the last few years has it reached Italy as a musical term.

Most musical instruments can stand phonetic translation,
though the cymbals ('cymbales' in French) are 'cinelli' (or more
recently 'piatti') in Italy and 'Becken' in German.

The disparity in the meaning of *piano* and *Klavier* has been
referred to on p. 141. Where accuracy warrants it, *piano* should
be translated to *Hammerklavier* (Beethoven preferred at one stage
the expression *Hammerklavier* to *Pianoforte*, and used it for his
op. 106) or to *Pianoforte* in German, and *Klavier* should be
translated to *keyboard instrument* in English.

If the expression 'Streichinstrumente' is used as the German
equivalent for stringed instrument, the harp is omitted. If the
harp is to be included, it has to be 'Saiteninstrumente', or
'Streicher und Harfe'.

The bassoon is a 'basson' in French, but in German and
Italian it is the 'Fagott(o)'. This word's English equivalent
'faggot', would be a reasonable English name for the instrument
as well, as the correct meaning of faggot is a 'bundle' of pieces
(usually wood). The bassoon is 'bundled' because it consists,

for convenience's sake, of parallel pipes. If it were not a 'faggot', it would have to be three or four yards long in order to reach its lower register and the counter bassoon would have to extend to a formidable twenty feet.

A selection of general musical terms, as well as a table of comparative notation terminology, an item especially liable to international misunderstandings, is given in the following table.

GENERAL MUSICAL TERMS

English and American		German	French	Italian
C		C	ut	do
C flat		ces	ut bémol	do bemolle
C sharp		cis	ut dièse	do diesis
D		D	re	re
E		E	mi	mi
F		F	fa	fa
G		G	sol	sol
A		A	la	la
B flat	Beware!	B	si bémol	si bemolle
B natural		H	si	si

NOTATION TERMINOLOGY

Great Britain and Commonwealth Countries Except Canada, S. Africa	America Austria Germany Canada	France	Italy
semibreve	whole (ganze) note	Ronde	semibreve
minim	1/2 note	Blanche	minima
crotchet	1/4 note	Noire	semiminima
quaver	1/8 note	Croche	croma
semiquaver	1/16 note	Double Croche	semicroma
demisemiquaver	1/32 note	Triple Croche	biscroma
hemidemisemiquaver	1/64 note	Quadruple Croche	semibiscroma

NINTH CHAPTER

MUSIC AND CRITIC

MUSIC AND CRITIC

It is very easy to criticize music. For reasons which are psychologically rather obscure, music provokes and elicits criticism almost reflex-like. Everyone criticizes music, and under certain circumstances it is probably easier to criticize music than to refrain from so doing.

To produce and write valid criticism about music is a different matter altogether and is, potentially, a public service of considerable importance. It is a service which not only interests those who read it, but also affects materially and sometimes even decisively those about whom it is written. A service which can be so perilous for those it affects must without doubt be executed in a very skilful manner, and the public is most definitely entitled to expect certain qualifications and qualities from those who are in a position to wield so dangerous a weapon.

A good critic must be:

1. KNOWLEDGEABLE. To have been trained as a professional musician is a great help, especially if composition and a good variety of instruments have been fully studied. However, it seems possible for people who have absorbed a large amount of music as a hobby to achieve a nearly equivalent experience. In order to criticize opera it is also relevant to have worked in an opera house, because the understanding of operatic presentation (and therefore the ability to analyse faults), is particularly difficult to acquire through a 'front of the house' experience only.

2. WELL EDUCATED. It is essential that he has learnt Latin and desirable that he should have learnt Greek. He must have a sound training in

classical history and ancient religion,* as well as in the history of the Renaissance and the history of Art. Our theatre is derived from the Greek theatre and retains many Greek expressions. The habitual misuse of terms like *protagonist* by the critics can prejudice the reader, even if unjustly, against the whole of the review's content. The critic should also know sufficient of the operatic languages to be able to read a libretto with the help of a dictionary.

3. ARTICULATE. He must be able to argue concisely, and yet with a relaxed, individual style. This demands both literary scholarship and journalistic training.

4. IMAGINATIVE. He must have ideas that make good reading, but must beware of the temptation to hang his own ideas on the hook of every possible performance.

5. INDUSTRIOUS. He must do his 'homework' before every performance and keep scrupulously up to date with performing trends and creative developments. This requires time as well as travel.

6. FORTUNATE. He must retain an exceptionally acute sense of hearing well into middle age: this requires good fortune, because soon after the age of thirty the perception of high pitched sounds begins to deteriorate and this deterioration can proceed fairly quickly and lead to 'perceptive' deafness. Good hearing for low sounds is generally much longer maintained.

7. ENTHUSIASTIC. His enjoyment of listening to music must be durable and persistent.

8. SYMPATHETIC. He must show understanding of technical and practical difficulties, and in order to retain this understanding he must, even if only intermittently, still participate *actively* in music-making. The level of his technical competence is not relevant but a permanent restriction to musical *passivity* inevitably leads to garbled and distorted views on musical problems. He must also be:

---

* Greek mythology and religion as well as ancient history still act as an inexhaustible fount of operatic subjects. Greek religion is the 'natural' religion of mankind and its impact was never fully lost. During the more fertile phases of man's artistic aspirations its fascination has frequently erupted into a quasi-acceptance of some of its customs, e.g. the pagan rites of the Renaissance, and it has influenced opera significantly.

9. GOOD-NATURED in wit and humour, and

10. RECEPTIVE to new ideas.

11. OPTIMISTIC. Even when he is tired, or bored (both are unavoidable happenings in this profession), he must not be tempted to give up.

Finally, he must be, and remain,

12. ABSOLUTELY INCORRUPTIBLE in Baccho, in Venere (utriusque generis!) et in auro.

Small wonder that those who command so formidable an array of qualifications are rare birds indeed—and always have been.

Music criticism appeared first of all in books, then in special music periodicals, and later still it reached the daily newspaper columns. It has gained little in the process, and bears the burden of a bad history. A so-called expert belaboured Bach with rather stupid criticism, while the congregation was more than pleased with their 'Thomas-Kantor'. A whole volume of half-witted criticisms of Wagner has been published. The most important music critic of his century, Eduard Hanslick, is now chiefly remembered for his wrong assessment of Wagner's music: little could he foresee that the character of Sixtus Beckmesser, which incorporated a travesty of his own personality (at one stage Richard Wagner intended to call this role Hans Lick), would so easily outlive his own fame.

The Germans, inclined to be systematic, even in the recollection of their errors, now possess an up-to-date dictionary of the blunders of musical critics and the perhaps rather misleadingly termed *Lexicon of Musical Invective** contains a good deal of interesting information of this type.

The right to express an opinion, and every editor's right to publish it, is of course unquestionable. The music critic's opinion is however, as soon as it appears in print, apt to be taken by the public as an authoritative judgment and not as a personal

---

* By N. Slonimsky (Univ. of Washington Press).

opinion. This is neither the fault of the critic nor the fault of his editor: it is the fault of a public which vacillates notoriously between accepting everything in black and white as gospel truth, and regarding anything which appears in the newspapers as *ipso facto* untrue.

The editors of those daily newspapers which cater for a vast readership, do not necessarily consider musical criticism an important subject. If a new film is being shown, it might eventually be seen by millions of people, all of whom are potentially interested in what the film critic has to say about it. Operatic criticism is virtually of interest only to those who see the performance, and this may well amount to less than ten thousand people for the whole of a production. A few other small groups of readers may be interested as well, but from the circulation point of view they remain an insignificant minority.

Music criticism can therefore do a popular newspaper not much good: it is unduly controversial and can only bring trouble. The best thing a fair-minded editor can do is to appoint a well-qualified person to the post. Best qualified to judge musical performances are obviously those whom study, knowledge and practical experience of the subject have made true experts. This points clearly to those who have the academic and practical training of the conductor, as the group of people from which the applicant should be chosen.

Insurmountable difficulties, however, prevent this logical conclusion from being put into practice. Conductors have become conductors because they like active music-making. They like to conduct, and may not be attracted to the work of the newspaper critic. They may, besides, be quite unable to write that quickly composed, readable journalistic prose which is expected of the critic. The main qualification in writing criticism of music is therefore a journalistic one, although some critics like to claim that they are 'musicians who have been seconded to journalism'.

Every music critic has been appointed to his post by the newspaper's proprietor or editor, because his or her employer thought that the applicant was competent to write about music, knew how to write well, and certainly knew how to write quickly. At the best of times it is not an easy matter to write with great dispatch, and the need to judge such difficult matters as artistic performances under extreme pressure makes the task even more difficult. The time available to the critic to express his views in well reasoned argument, can frequently be measured in minutes rather than in hours: at the most it is one and a half hours for five hundred words or so.

Most writers change and rechange everything they write many times, and never let anything go into print which they have not 'slept on' and reconsidered. The newspaper critic seldom has a chance to reconsider anything. Pressure of time does not, of course, apply to the weekly newspapers, nor to the music or opera periodicals, though they do not really seem to benefit from this advantage.

Although neither the newspaper's editor nor its proprietor is likely to be competent to evaluate the musical qualifications of their candidate, they have occasionally picked winners. It is amusing to reflect that one of the best music critics, Bernard Shaw, was offered the post because it seemed to his editor* that this was the best way to 'get rid of his politics'. It is not likely that he knew the details of Bernard Shaw's very sound musical training, but in any case not many editors' choices can prove so spectacularly successful. In practice, the appointment of critic on the 'popular' and provincial newspapers is usually given to capable journalists who are known to be very fond of music, and all music critics are indeed undoubtedly very fond of music. The results of their subsequent activities, however, are often such as those which we can expect if the qualification to judge at the Dublin Horse Show would be 'to be very fond of horses'.

If the critic's sincere love for music is not in doubt, his

---

* The Star's 'Tay Pay O'Connor'.

rather personal attitude towards it cannot be doubted either. If a baronetcy should be awarded to a music critic, involving the obligation to select a suitable motto, he may well choose 'I know what I like'. The bias which results from his perfectly honest, but rather personal views and from his predilections, in combination with the fact that any chink in his armour, any little weakness, can lead him a long way in the wrong direction, presents the real problem.

The criticized, too, can be faulted for their attitude. In conformity with human nature, they are quite pleased to accept extravagant praise even if they know it to be undeserved. They are, particularly the recital artists, eager to use such praise for their own publicity purposes, thus repaying the publicity which they have received with publicity for the paper and the critic. On the other hand, they are inclined to feel unduly irritated and hurt by 'vicious' attacks. They fail to appreciate that the requirements of readability necessitate dramatization and exaggeration at both ends in order to prevent musical criticism from becoming very dull reading matter, and that all attempts to make it livelier are prone to make it hurtful or inaccurate.

The full-time music critic does certainly not have a very amusing life. To have to sit night after night through performances which may be dull, or just outside the sphere of his real interest in music, can be punishing. The variety of the fare which is on offer increases the effort. He is expected to write about Monteverdi one night, Stockhausen the next, then Wagner—all with equal knowledge and enjoyment. It is not surprising that after several years of such exertions, music critics can feel that they have not been appointed, but that they were indeed sentenced to their posts. In this country their conditions are especially severe—appreciably more so than in the United States. The critic is supposed to attend four or even five events during any one week: this presents working circumstances which by themselves form likely causes of chronic liver upsets.

It is very doubtful whether it is in anyone's interest to make criticism of music a permanent rather than, on principle, a temporary job. Debussy, who worked for some years as a music critic, is said to have held definite views on this point.*

It all adds up to the sad realization that ideal criticism, expertly done by experts on music, and presented with the chronicler's classical obligation of *sine ira et studio*, is almost impossible to write and may well be unexciting to read. Though doubts regarding the integrity of music critics have been expressed elsewhere, the integrity of London's critics has never been seriously questioned. Nevertheless, it must be realized that the vast majority of singers and musicians regard the present system of daily music criticism as a failure, and are convinced that it is artistically so inaccurate that it does not serve a serious purpose.

The position is, in their eyes, further aggravated by the fact that they are unable to correct any inaccuracy, falsehood or even blunder which may be contained in a review, whereas if the critic himself enters the field of operatic endeavour, things are quite different. If a critic, for argument's sake, translates the libretto of an opera and other critics take him to task, he will be able to reply to his detractors and argue his case. The singer is unable to do so: his only means for the correction of a misstatement is a letter to the paper's editor, but the chances of such a letter appearing in print are minimal. Legal proceedings are practically impossible. Even if an artist is convinced that a critic persistently writes in a malicious manner about him, actual malice would be almost impossible to prove in court. Moreover, if a critic is *invited* to attend a performance for the purposes of reviewing it, court proceedings based upon this review are virtually ruled out by law.

The ultimate appreciation of a work or of a performance is

---

* In pre-war Paris musical circles, a persistent rumour had it that a Debussy essay on musical criticism as a permanent career, with strong arguments against it, had been accidently mislaid in a publisher's office and could not be traced in spite of searches. The firm's offices disappeared during the war and the essay—if it existed—must be regarded as lost.

not that of the critics or 'experts', but is the result of a mysterious interaction between the work, its creator, the interpreters, and the interested part of the community.

Contemporary music has, at least at first hearing, often been misjudged by the critics. Great performers, too, are all too often not recognized early enough. This is particularly sad as, at the beginning of a career, and similarly at the occasion of a first performance in a new town, unduly severe comments can have grave consequences for a singer, and ruin his career.

Such considerations must, of course, not prevent a critic from expressing his honest opinion. However, history has proved many of these honest opinions about music to have been mistaken, and expert opinions have on the whole not fared better than the rest. Even the greatest of musicians have committed terrible blunders when they tried their hand at musical criticism. What Wagner wrote about Mendelssohn, what Tschaikowsky and Hugo Wolf had to say about Brahms, what Brahms had to say about Bruckner, and what Stravinsky had to say about Beethoven and Debussy about Strauss, matches perfectly the stuff which many of their colleagues *in critica* turn out at the present.

Some of the newspapers with quality readership employ music critics whose musicianship is indisputably of a high order, and a past organ-scholar of a famous college has gained himself almost universal respect. However, the truly just, correct and sensible music criticism is extremely difficult to achieve, because the acoustic sensation is so fleeting.

The criticism of pictorial art or of literature is produced under very different circumstances, because the critic can reflect, can look again, assess and compare. Critical assessment of recorded music too, may for this reason prove to be much more accurate, and may well be of lasting value. The music services of the radio systems have made notable beginnings in this respect.

The newspaper's music critic attempts the almost impossible with, for obvious reasons, inadequate means. It is churlish to take critics to task because today's reviews of yesterday's performance almost invariably contradict one another. Equally churlish is it to harp on these differences. However, they can be quite legitimately used to score the following three points:

1. Criticism of musical events express a personal opinion which must not be taken for a conclusive judgment.

2. The writing of immediate, valid criticism of musical events has only very rarely been accomplished in the past, and is most likely to remain an aim which cannot regularly be fulfilled.

3. In fleeting sensations, the personal element of liking or of disliking is so powerful, that in spite of considerable experience, it permits one to rave—or to condemn—with equal justification and with sincere conviction.

This, of course, finally proves only one thing, i.e. that the instant 'judging' of performed music is absurdly difficult, and that its inconsistencies and contradictions therefore reduce it too often to a sort of joke—though for some this may be a very painful one. On the whole, jokes no doubt are good things— as long as they are not taken seriously!

As far as the public is concerned, the newspaper critic is an entertainer and not an instructor. The critical approach to music can at the best of times, help or guide our understanding only in a very limited way.

Goethe's famous words that "we ourselves must win what we have inherited from our forebears, in order that we may own it" apply to music as well. The critic can neither save us effort, nor can we use him as a short-cut to knowledge. Knowledge must be acquired, and must be used in conjunction with unaffected sincerity in order to enable us to perceive music in the way in which Beethoven defined it: the incomparable mingling of the spiritual with the sensual.

Index of Names and Works